RENAULT F1

1977 - 1997

Beyond the Yellow Teapot

British GP,
14 July 1977

Gareth Rogers

RENAULT F1

1977 - 1997

Beyond the Yellow Teapot

TEMPUS

To my nephew, Chris Rogers. First of the next generation and a fellow Formula One fan.

First published 2005

Tempus Publishing Ltd
The Mill, Brimscombe Port
Stroud, Gloucestershire GL5 2QG
www.tempus-publishing.com

British Library Cataloguing in Publication Data.
A catalogue record for this book is available from the British Library.

ISBN 0 7524 3553 1

Typesetting, design and origination by Tempus Publishing.
Printed in Great Britain

Contents

Preface

At the beginning of the twentieth century, when the automobile was still very much in its infancy, Louis and Marcel Renault counted among the most prominent of motor racing's early pioneers, taking their first victory – the 1899 Paris to Rambuillet road race – at the wheel of an A-type voiturette. Later, between 1920 and 1930 Renault scored a fine series of rallying successes and continued to compete on a regular basis during the post-Second World War years.

In the 1960s, with the introduction of the Renault 8 Gordini Cup, the French manufacturer was the first to promote the idea of a single-make series, a concept followed up by a Formula Renault Championship shortly afterwards. Both these competitions were recognised as career springboards for talented young drivers such as future World Champion Alain Prost.

The founding in 1975 of Renault Sport saw the marque's competition activities enter a new era. Two years later the first Renault Formula One car was unveiled. Although the Formula One programme swiftly became a priority, the company's commitment to rallying and its promotional formulas was consolidated with the creation of separate Rallies and Sports Promotions departments. Today Renault is one of the few manufacturers to have an active presence at all levels of competition, all the way from the Renault Elf Campus Cup, reserved for young drivers from sixteen to nineteen years of age, to Formula One.

In 1997 Renault celebrated twenty years of involvement in Formula One and, in the same year, took the decision to take a break from the sport. Ever since its debut in July 1977 Renault has greatly influenced the sport. It started out with its own team (1977-1985) when it revolutionised engine technology by introducing supercharging. This technique was afterwards copied by all its competitors. Then, in 1987, it imposed the V10 configuration as the norm for naturally aspirated engines in Formula One. Thanks to the exceptional reliability, sheer power and flexibility of the famous RS engines, Renault won, with the Williams and Benetton teams, many honours. Six Constructors' World Championship titles (1992, 1993, 1994, 1995, 1996 and 1997) and five Drivers' World Championship titles with Nigel Mansell (1992), Alain Prost (1993), Michael Schumacher (1995), Damon Hill (1996) and Jacques Villeneuve (1997) were achieved.

Over a century, from the Renault brothers' first triumph in 1899, the six consecutive Formula One world titles plus a World Rallying title in 1973 and victory in the Le Mans 24-Hours in 1978, Renault has risen to the challenge of creating and innovating new techniques. In doing so it has demonstrated indisputably the technological expertise and competence of its engineers and technicians.

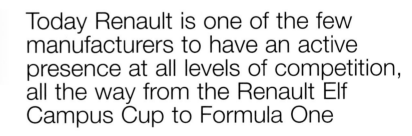

Today Renault is one of the few manufacturers to have an active presence at all levels of competition, all the way from the Renault Elf Campus Cup to Formula One

RS1 with the Renault Sport team, 9 May 1977

Trials, 31 May 1977

Chapter One:
Renault Frères

Renault Formula One enjoyed a relaunch into Grand Prix racing as the twenty-first century began to unfold – but the seeds of its motor sport culture were planted as the nineteenth century ended.

Competition was an important element in Renault's philosophy when the company was established by Louis, Marcel and Fernard Renault in 1899. Louis was the engineer and at the age of eleven he designed an electric lighting system for his bedroom. At fourteen he began to tinker with a Panhard engine and, when he finished his military service in 1898, he built his first car in a shed at the end of the garden of the Renault family house in the Paris suburb of Billancourt. This was powered by a De Dion Bouton engine but the chassis was designed by Louis and the major innovation was that it featured a drive-shaft transmission rather than the normal chain-driven system.

On 24 December 1898 the twenty-year-old Louis was spending Christmas Eve with some friends. Confident about his invention, he bet them that his A-type voiturette could climb the thirteen per cent slope of the Rue Lepic in Montmarte. Not only was Louis' gamble successful, he also accepted twelve cash deposits for firm orders. A few months later he filed the patent for the direct-drive system that would make his fortune. It was soon adopted by all the contemporary car manufacturers.

His two brothers set up The Renault Brothers Company in 1899. Interestingly, Marcel and Fernard were the shareholders; Louis was only paid a salary while he proved there was a future in automobiles.

It was through racing that 'Société Renault Frères' became known, with Louis and Marcel at the wheels of their vehicles. In the summer of 1899 they entered cars in the Paris-Trouville race and Louis won the light-car class. After that the order book grew and, over a six-month period, their newly recruited production team built sixty cars. During 1900 a further 179 were to be assembled.

Renault's early racing success was with class wins in the city-to-city races including Paris-Bordeaux, Paris-Ostend, Paris-Berlin and, most significantly, the Paris-Vienna in June 1902. After a couple of years' success the company had become strong enough to plan for its own engines and had hired one of the De Dion Boulton engine designers. He produced the first Renault engine for this epic race in which Renault entered three cars. It was built to a design of brilliant simplicity. The engine speed was capped at 1,100rpm and a special device made it possible to increase the engine power by twenty per cent for short spurts. Technology had already entered Renault history! The entry was huge with 118 cars and speeds in the early part of the event as high as 70mph. The small-engine Renaults could not match the pace but they proved to be more reliable than the bigger machines, notably over the mountain sections where the opposition broke down or even crashed out. With the other main contenders either delayed or retired, Marcel Renault was the first man to make it to Vienna, only twelve minutes ahead of Henri Farman's Panhard! It was a famous victory and a marvellous marketing exercise. Business boomed. The company expanded rapidly and the workshops in Paris were forced to expand to 7,500 square metres.

There was now a Renault range, including the first saloon car. That first Renault engine had four cylinders and horsepower of 24. At this time – and significantly for our story – Louis patented the first turbo.

Ferenc Szisz
(Renault AK) leads
the 1906 French
Grand Prix

Louis was the engineer and at the age of eleven he designed an electric lighting system for his bedroom

Racing was gaining in popularity and the entry for the next major event, the 1903 Paris-Madrid, was an enormous 275 vehicles. Then tragedy struck.

On the first day there were a series of accidents and a dozen of them led to fatalities. Marcel crashed when he went off the road at Angoulême near Poitiers. Louis Renault was second when the race reached Bordeaux and the organisers took the decision to cancel the event. Two days later Marcel died of his injuries. He was thirty-one. Louis had lost a brother and a most loyal supporter in his quest. He gave up racing for good and handed to professional drivers the task of furthering the Renault cause not just in France but in the Americas and Africa. Eventually an international sales network would accompany these competitive endeavours.

Fate was now to play a positive hand for, in 1905, Louis agreed to build another racing machine. The new vehicle took its place in the annals of motor sport history when Louis's former co-driver, Ferenc Szisz, won the inaugural Grand Prix de l'ACF in 1906. The event was regarded as the first real 'Grand Prix'. A three-car team of Ferenc Szisz, Claude Richez and Jean Edmond were supplied with cars, with Szisz finishing second the following year in the Grand Prix de l'ACF in Dieppe. Szisz continued in 1908 but without success. That year Fernard Renault died after a long illness. He had already sold his stake in the company to his brother and it was renamed The Louis Renault Automobile Company. At thirty-two Louis was alone at the helm and expanding into other ventures. He was the first car manufacturer to move into aeronautics. Thereafter, Renault was not seen in Grand Prix racing for seventy years.

The company, under Louis's direction, expanded dramatically during the inter-war years but Louis was forced to put his factories into production for German armaments after the invasion of France in 1940. After the liberation Louis was arrested on a charge of collaboration and died in prison in late 1944 before having the chance to defend his name – a sad end to a lifetime of glorious achievement. As a result of his death the Renault company became national property and one of the leading car manufacturers in the world.

Renault avoided competition until one of its dealers, Jean Redele, established the Alpine tuning business and began preparing Renault products for rallying. This developed in the 1950s and Alpine-tuned Dauphines later won the Tour de Corse and the Monte Carlo Rally. It was not until the late 1960s that Renault began to consider car racing and set up the Renault 8 Gordini Cup, which stimulated the growth of French motor sport. There were ambitions in several directions and the beginning of concepts that would eventually lead to the very apex of motor racing.

The Alpine Renault team targeted victory in their class in the Le Mans 24-Hours, where thermal efficiency and performance were the criteria. However, the ordinary R8 was suddenly seen in a new light by fans. It appeared as a racing machine with distinctive blue bodywork reflecting its nationality and two white stripes that reached the back bumpers from the front of the bonnet. It was a 'souped-up' version too! It became known as the R8 Gordini. Soon the visual image became even more positive as the racers were spectacular and successful on track. More tellingly, the Coupe Gordini was the opportunity for a new generation of drivers. The most talented of the first crop were to reach the pinnacle of Formula One, including Jean-Pierre Jabouille, who was to play such a significant part in the Renault Formula One story.

A500 prototype
December 1976

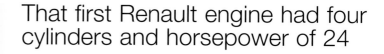

That first Renault engine had four cylinders and horsepower of 24

The impetus was now there for drivers to be developed through the formulae with the benefit of fame and success being integrated with the Renault marque. Among those in the ranks to compete in a Formula Renault series, launched in 1971, were Alain Prost, Rene Arnoux, Jacques Lafitte, Didier Pironi, Patrick Tambay and, of course, Jean-Pierre Jabouille.

There was parallel success in the European Rally Championship of 1970 and the World Rally Championship of 1971. The feat was repeated at that level in 1973. Then the 2-litre sports car programme resulted in European Championship success in 1974. In 1975 Renault took over Gordini and the Renault-Gordini operations were amalgamated as Renault Sport at Viry-Chatillon in the suburbs of Paris. In 1976 the first fruit was borne as Jean-Pierre Jabouille gave Renault victory in the European Formula Two Championship.

Already, on the initiative of Jean Teramorsi, Renault had taken up a new challenge in secret: Formula One. In 1975, with strict security, Renault Sport started to develop the Renault Gordini V6 turbocharged engine. No car manufacturer in Formula One had ever taken such a gamble. Simultaneously, Alpine was building a single-seater, the first chassis of its kind, at the Dieppe plant. On 23 March 1976 the prototype was taken through its paces at the Michelin track at Clermont-Ferrand. Behind the wheel, inevitably, was Jean-Pierre Jabouille. By May the company was ready to make an announcement. It did unveil its prototype, known as the A500, claiming that it was only an experimental single seater, a 'laboratory on wheels' that would never be entered in competition. Despite that public utterance the parent company was, in July, to give the green light for the creation of a full-time racing stable. The great adventure had begun!

A 'laboratory on wheels'

Chapter Two:
The Yellow Teapot

The decision to take part in the World Formula One Championship of 1977 was not an easy one. Certain members of the board were against it. They believed that Renault's presence would be doing more for the promotion of the driver than the marque itself. However Bernard Hanon, the managing director of the automobile division, was one of those most strongly in favour of an involvement in Formula One: 'We had been working on a turbo engine for some years and it was time to take the plunge. Only active participation in races could provide us with the sort of experience we needed to apply our technology to the production car which was the ultimate aim of involvement.'

There were a great many problems to overcome but Renault took up its new challenge with enthusiasm, even if they knew they were hardly going to stage an upset in a season dominated by Niki Lauda of Ferrari, who went on to win his second title. Although Jean-Pierre Jabouille had reservations about Renault's plans to introduce a small-capacity turbocharged engine into Formula One, he had been prepared to track test since 1976. It was a black prototype single-seater that emitted a whistling noise when the engine was running. The chassis was experimental but many features were carried forward to the RS 101, launched in 1977. Jabouille was the obvious choice for that magic maiden voyage at the British Grand Prix at Silverstone on Bastille Day – 14 July.

When the newcomer made its debut in practice, the Formula One world sniggered. Yellow in colour, badged with a big Renault diamond and the Elf logo, the RS 101 not only whistled but steamed like a teapot! Jabouille, however, had a reputation for knowing how to set up and develop a car: 'Everybody was working very hard. We all believed in the project, but nobody knew how long it would take to get it working.' The result of the sleepless nights was a light alloy monocoque with a stressed engine and gearbox. The engine was a ninety-degree V6 with a capacity of 1,492cc, four valves per cylinder and was fed by a single turbo. The turbo was chosen as a tried and tested technology following Renault's successful prototype programme and also for economic reasons.

A difficult beginning was experienced at Silverstone as Jabouille explains: 'Before we even had time to find a baseline set-up, the turbo broke. We quickly realised the problem was coming from the excessive temperatures generated by the exhausts. Some minor developments, which seemed beneficial in isolation, actually worked against us when they were put together.' This race and those in Holland, Italy and the Eastern USA were not completed. The Renault engineers were convinced their choice was well founded, and solved the difficulties one by one. 'Problems with the intercooler meant the engine was overheating, and we were holing pistons regularly. Oil was dropping onto the exhausts and turbo, which were already operating at a temperature of around 900 degrees centigrade. Smoke and flames were almost guaranteed,' recalls Jabouille, who had to play firefighter when it happened. 'I used to get calmly out of the car, and stuff one of my gloves down the exhaust. The fire stopped immediately.'

Jabouille also commented on the adoption of style required at the time: 'When we first started running the car the throttle lag was terrifying. Full power arrived well after you had put the accelerator to the floor. The first time I tried the car, I seriously wondered how we were going to be able to make a success of it.'

Trials pit stop, 11 May 1976

Yellow in colour, badged with a big Renault diamond and the Elf logo, the RS 101 not only whistled but steamed like a teapot!

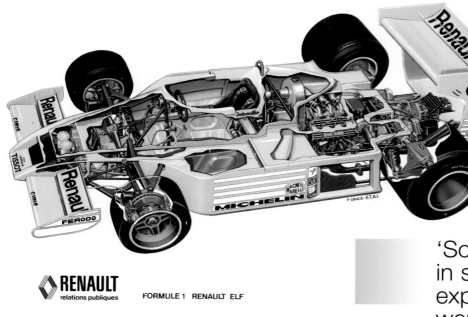

Renault RS01 cutaway
diagram, 1978

RENAULT
relations publiques

FORMULE 1 RENAULT ELF

'Sometimes, the power came in suddenly, much earlier than expected. When that happened, you were spinning before you knew it!'

Renault had succeeded with a 2-litre turbo, but reducing the capacity to 1.5 litres gave them problems. 'You had to get on the throttle very early. Sometimes it worked. Sometimes, the power came in suddenly, much earlier than expected. When that happened, you were spinning before you knew it! On the other hand, when I took my foot off the throttle, the car carried on going for a brief moment. Honestly, we didn't expect things to be so complicated but, having said that, we began winning in 1979. Lots of teams would dream of that just a season and a half after their debut.'

Jabouille's attention to detail allowed him to thoroughly brief the engineers and also make them understand that the power had to be available in a broad, flexible band. The driver also noted – for future reference – that when Renault arrived in the pits they still remained the source of amusement for other teams as his mechanics struggled with the unpredictable engines. However, with Jabouille's determination and his collaboration with Gerard Larousse, the technical director of Renault Sport, progress was made race by race. Larousse had been invited by Bernard Hanon

to take charge of shaping Renault's motor sport activities at the beginning of the same year that Jabouille began testing the Formula One model. It was a radical move at that time to appoint an ex-rally driver to head up the competition department with a new emphasis on circuit racing. However, it proved an inspired move. Recently retired from action behind the wheel, Gerard Larousse was immediately thrown into the deep end, as he had to ratify the newly created Renault Sport's decision to pursue Formula One. A man suited for an adventure, he also combined his flair with a focus on organisation and operation. He had an obsessive eye for detail, which earned him few friends but much success. Despite responsibility for the company's involvement in the Le Mans 24-Hours, he had to thrust the Formula One commitment through simultaneously. A research department was built at the Viry-Chatillon factory and Larousse was unflinching in his belief in the concept of turbocharging.

Despite the derision, Larousse would prove the master in time!

Debut for a turbocharged engine in
a Grand Prix, Silverstone practice
14 July 1977

British GP, 16 July 1977

Chapter Three:
The First Harvest

For Renault, the 1978 season was one of numerous retirements, and a sporting effort split between Formula One and the Le Mans 24-Hours. This meant the team didn't start a Grand Prix until South Africa, the third race of the season. Jean-Pierre Jabouille was again the team's sole driver. He scored the car's first finish at Monaco and even scored points at Watkins Glen, USA. Jean-Pierre came in fourth behind Carlos Reuteman, Alan Jones and Jody Scheckter. The 1.5-litre turbocharged V6 had undergone major modifications during the year, notably a mixed air/water cooling system adopted for the Austrian Grand Prix, plus new pistons and piston rings.

There was still a taste of adventure in the air for the second season in Formula One as the team strove to make the car reliable. Gerard Larousse recalls: 'We were still getting to grips with the sport and continued to suffer a good many problems. Jabouille qualified well and put in good times when the car was cold. However, we hit trouble as soon as the temperatures on the intercoolers rose. We were steadily building up our expertise in small-engine-capacity turbo technology but a great deal of work lay in store. We weren't spared problems on the chassis side either. The English, who had significantly more experience than us in this domain, would smile when we turned up at races. When we finished our first GP, then scored our first points, it came as a big relief.'

While Jean-Pierre Jabouille was bringing home the Renault for due reward after his years of toil, the Renault management were also paying attention to the on-track endeavours of a former protégé – Rene Arnoux. Arnoux had demonstrated his capacity to make good use of modest equipment in a debut season primarily with Surtees but initially with Martini. Before racing in Formula One, Arnoux had been victorious in Formula Renault, Formula Renault Europe and Formula Two. Now he was invited to return to the fold as the parent company began to prepare to invest in a two-racer team after an eighteen-month initiation period.

Jean-Pierre Jabouille's career had been a mixed one but at Dijon-Prenois on 1 July 1979 justice was done for all his tenacity and dedication to the Renault cause. The Frenchman began the race by going easy on his tyres, allowing Gilles Villeneuve's Ferrari to escape. Then, on lap forty-seven, Jean-Pierre caught and passed the Ferrari for the lead and the win. Surely on home soil there could never have been a better context in which to receive such a wonderful result with Rene Arnoux only just being pipped to second place by Villeneuve after a classic wheel-to-wheel battle at the climax of the race. On the podium Jabouille's tears flowed freely. The great breakthrough – and a place in history for himself and his team – had come.

After that great day, Renault's strong performances continued with a front-row grid position for Jabouille and second in the race

Monaco GP, 7 May 1978 *(Right)*

Podium, French GP, 1 July 1979 *(Below)*

for Arnoux in Great Britain. These were followed by pole position in Germany for Jabouille and poles in Austria and Holland for Arnoux. Finally, in Monza, the front row was 100 per cent Renault.

With twenty-six points, Renault finished sixth in the Constructors' World Championship, just ahead of McLaren. The Drivers' World Championship was won by Jody Scheckter for Ferrari. Rene Arnoux finished eighth with Jean-Pierre Jabouille thirteenth.

The final word rests with the team leader: 'This was my third season with Renault and development work over the winter had proved very fruitful. We knew the car was capable of winning but couldn't know exactly when the first victory would come. The early part of the season confirmed our faith. In South Africa I started a GP from pole position for the first time in the team's short history. The next big step came in France. We had covered race distance without the slightest problem two weeks beforehand and we knew the car was ripe for a top result. The race itself went like a dream. Between us, Rene and I were fastest in qualifying, set the fastest lap and won outright.'

Overall, Renault had finished the 1978 season twelfth in the Constructors' World Championship, with three points. The following year was to see a transformation for Jabouille and Arnoux. This pair were distinctive in their personalities and this made for a fascinating brew. Jabouille perfected his set-up before venturing on track and opening up. Arnoux just jumped in the car and rode his luck. Once in the yellow Renault, Arnoux displayed a marvellous turn of speed and paid scant regard to the contribution of Jabouille both on and off track. This did not have the foundation of a happy working relationship between the drivers but in the final analysis Renault's primary concern was the potential for the pair to achieve success.

After the dominance of the Lotus in 1978 the Ligier JS11, equipped with a Cosworth V8 engine, was the car to beat, Jacques Lafitte winning the first two races. At Kyalami, South Africa, Renault finally showed their strength, with Jean-Pierre

Jabouille securing the team's first pole position. Even though the Renault car still had no ground-effect, it was equipped with Michelin tyres on a circuit that favoured traction over aerodynamic grip. Also, at that sort of high altitude caused the Renault turbo engine lost less power than the normally aspirated engines of its rivals. The French engine generated 460 horsepower to the Cosworth's 410. Unfortunately, however, it rained during the race and Jabouille could not take advantage of his turbo engine.

In Spain, Renault finally introduced ground-effect on the RS10. The chassis became more and more balanced and in Monaco the engine was given a double-turbo system. Every line of cylinders had its own turbo and the engine gained 1,200rpm. The new turbos, supplied by KKK, were much smaller. A few weeks later the team won outright. Nobody ever dared call the Renault the 'Yellow Teapot' again.

Engine, February 1978 *(above)*

Podium, British GP, 14 July 1979 *(right)*

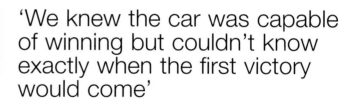

'We knew the car was capable of winning but couldn't know exactly when the first victory would come'

Viry Chatillon factory,
November 1979

Chapter Four:
On Cruising Speed

Renault made much progress with the turbo in the close season leading into 1980. Carbon fibre components for the fuel tank, an improved power-train assembly (five speeds instead of six) and other new developments brought a gain of around 30kg. The car weighed 605kg. The bodywork was now in Kevlar, not fibreglass, and had been the object of sustained work in the wind tunnel. On the engine side, the valve springs and cylinder heads had been strengthened.

The new decade heralded a new car in reality – the RE20 125. The Renault Sport designation had been changed to Renault Elf, marking their allegiance to their major backer and long-term technical partner. Rene Arnoux proved to be the quicker of the two drivers but Jean-Pierre Jabouille could still claim two poles for 1980. The first was the second race of the season in Brazil but it was Arnoux who took the win after Jabouille retired with turbo failure. The winning car ran out of fuel just a few metres after the finish line. Rene's second win came in the next race at Kyalami in the thin air of the South African highlands – ideally suited to turbo engines. This meant total Renault domination. Pole-sitter Jabouille led the first sixty-one laps before he suffered a puncture on one of his Michelin radials. Arnoux overtook his teammate to take a dominating win and lead the World Championship aggregates. However, the rest of the season saw technical problems at many races but Renault did finish fourth in the Constructors' World Championship. After those victories in Brazil and South Africa, Rene Arnoux took pole in Austria, Holland and Italy. Jean-Pierre Jabouille also took a win at Zeltweg, where the effectiveness of the Michelin tyres allowed the Renaults to run less downforce. The pair also achieved the front-row grids at Zandvoort and Monza.

Sadly, the team's great pioneer was to suffer a major crash at Montreal. Jabouille hit a barrier head on at 140mph and suffered seven fractures of the right leg. The cause of the crash was diagnosed as a faulty wishbone. He was not replaced at Watkins Glen and Arnoux drove alone. Arnoux amassed twenty points in total and was sixth in the final championship standings. The reliability of Williams provided Alan Jones with five wins and the world title. Jean-Pierre Jabouille never drove for Renault again but his contribution to that team's cause is immortal.

An inside perspective on that season is provided by Pierre Dupasquier, who was responsible for Michelin's Formula One programme: 'For Renault, 1980 was a further year of learning. The car continued to progress, but there was still some way to go until full reliability was reached. We succeeded in getting a good match between the tyres and the chassis when the car evolved aerodynamically. I must say we surprised ourselves. It was a difficult year as far as research was concerned and we progressed in small steps. In the process we gleaned, however, a whole host of data which would serve over the following years. It was thanks to the experience obtained that we were able to supply the whole grid the following season. I would go so far as to say that the tyres which are on the market today benefit directly from the association between Michelin and Renault of that era.'

V6 turbo engine

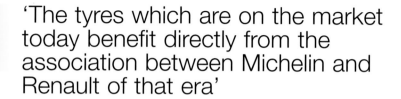

'The tyres which are on the market today benefit directly from the association between Michelin and Renault of that era'

Jean-Pierre Jabouille, Brazilian GP, 27 January 1980

Brazilian GP, 27 January 1980

If a creative tension had existed in the Renault camp between Jabouille and Arnoux, the atmosphere reached a new dimension with the acquisition of Alain Prost for 1981. Prost had been given his first Formula One drives by McLaren the previous season. This stint with the British team was a modest foundation for a driver who was eventually to prove France's greatest ever driver and one of the sport's most outstanding World Champions. McLaren were not in the same shape as the glory days in which the team had seen Emerson Fittipaldi and James Hunt reach the heights. This served to prove Prost's talent as, in an uncompetitive car, the diminutive Frenchman scored a point on his debut. Gerard Larrousse began to monitor the performances of his young compatriot. When Jean-Pierre Jabouille had to re-assess his future, Renault's technical director had no hesitation in offering Prost a deal. Although contracted to McLaren, the appeal of driving for a French team was overwhelming. He sought legal advice and support to ensure his availability for Renault.

Alain Prost was returning home in more ways than one. Like Rene Arnoux, he had been a winner in the junior ranks. He had worked closely with the team on technical feedback to ensure a competitive unit to take him to the European Formula Three title. Renault recognised his maturity and fine racing brain. He had the ability to sustain the contribution that Jean-Pierre Jabouille had brought to Renault Formula One development as a test driver. As the 1981 season progressed Prost began to outpace Arnoux. Rene, who possessed so much natural speed, was surprised to see the younger driver quickly developing into the calculating driver Larrousse had already recognised. Renault struggled with their updated 1980 cars but, when the new RE30 came along, matters looked up. Soon Prost became the de facto number-one driver. He scored three wins and led most laps of all during the season. His first major breakthrough would remarkably mirror that of the ultimate Renault hero Jabouille – on home soil at Dijon. He also led for 1,073.4km in the season while Rene Arnoux scored

no wins and eleven points, having led for 278.9km in comparison. In qualifying Prost outscored Arnoux by a ratio of 2:1. Of these, however, Arnoux had four poles compared to two set by Prost. However, Prost finished with forty-three points – only seven behind World Champion Nelson Piquet!

**Podium,
South African GP,
1 March 1980**

Larousse was now faced with a management challenge of a size that matched the massive egos and fiery temperaments of his two charges

Itallian GP, 14 September 1980.
Jean-Pierre Jabouille and Rene Arnoux sandwich Carlos
Reutemann's Williams into the first turn

In essence the duo forged an excellent racing team for Renault Formula One but Larousse was now faced with a management challenge of a size that matched the massive egos and fiery temperaments of his two charges! One of them – Rene Arnoux – summed up the technical implications for the parent company by the end of the season: 'Our bet had been won. Nobody doubted the potential of the turbo principle any longer and certain teams began to copy our lead. The Renault engine was fantastic. It was powerful. Turbo lag was very, very short and it had plenty of power at low revs. Everything was perfect. No longer were we forced out with things like broken blocks or turbos, only by problems with ancillary parts, which we set about making reliable. Occasionally Prost and I would ask the engineers if they honestly thought we would finish by winning through. Their powers of persuasion ended up by stemming our doubts. I don't think I have ever raced with a team in which the driving inner flame has burned so intensely.'

**Podium,
Argentinian GP,
12 April 1981**
(above)

**Tests, February
1981** *(right)*

Rene Arnoux, British GP, 18 July 1981

Chapter Five:
So Near and Yet So Far

The highly competitive 1982 season was similar to 1981 for Renault but it was apparent that Arnoux was being demoted to the second-string position. Renault had noted that Prost had real potential but felt Arnoux was erratic. Prost immediately repaid their faith when he won the first two races of the season in South Africa and Brazil. In qualifying, Arnoux was on par with Prost as they ended the season at eight apiece with five poles for each driver. The Renault was now so developed it could even achieve pole on slower tracks like Monaco.

A mid-season slump meant that after the initial wins Prost didn't score a point for the next seven races. Arnoux's record was even worse and, after an initial podium place at Kyalami, he didn't score for nine races. Their home Grand Prix at the Paul Ricard circuit was now crucial for Renault and the French drivers. In qualifying Rene set pole with Alain second. With his eighteen championship points Prost was still in the hunt for the World title so Renault decided that, should the opportunity arise, team orders would take place. Proving he was no team player, Arnoux disregarded instructions as he was determined to win his home Grand Prix. There was total dismay in the Renault camp that day. Soon Rene Arnoux was negotiating his exit to Ferrari.

An all-Renault front row at the final race in Las Vegas completed the campaign. Prost finished fourth and Arnoux retired. In a season with the remarkable tally of eleven individual winners, Keke Rosberg of Williams was able to claim the title despite only a single win. Rosberg had a total of forty-four points with Prost in fourth place on thirty-four points. Jean Sage, Renault Sport's team manager, offered an insight into a frustrating season with the title eluding their number one driver again: 'The season got off to a good start. Perhaps too good. Prost won the first two races and Kylami was certainly the best of his career. The season continued with a series of pole positions but the car lacked reliability once again. Notably there was a persistent problem with an injection pump motor. One other serious problem was the rivalry between

Arnoux and Prost, which came to a head during the French Grand Prix. Arnoux forgot his responsibilities and, in spite of team orders, refused to let Prost through even though Alain was better placed in the championship. We thought for one moment we had a chance for the title. But it escaped us once again.'

South African GP, 29 January 1982 (above)

Starting grid, French GP, 17 April 1983 (right)

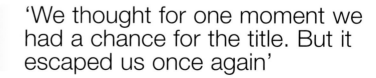

'We thought for one moment we had a chance for the title. But it escaped us once again'

As the atmosphere warmed up in the Renault garage we can see that the performances did as well. Finally Arnoux decided to join Ferrari following two years of a hot-and-cold relationship with Prost. He did eventually return to a working relationship with Renault in 1986 as a driver with Ligier, powered by a V6 turbo.

For the 1983 season Prost was joined by Eddie Cheever who, although an American national, had actually been brought up in Italy and progressed through that country's motor sport scene. The team also decided to supply engines to a second team, Lotus, for whom Nigel Mansell and Elio De Angelis drove. It was, however, only in the British Grand Prix that four Renault engines competed in the same race as Nigel Mansell had opted to remain with Ford power until then.

Meanwhile Cheever was finding out about life in the shadow of Alain Prost. Eddie had joined Renault from Ligier after a range of back-of-the-grid experiences with teams such as Theodore, Hesketh and Osella before moving up to Tyrrell and Ligier. Gerard Larousse knew Cheever would be supportive of Prost's world title aspirations but the American's own results proved disappointing. He was given the same equipment and set-up as his French teammate but made only a limited number of podium appearances. He seemed resigned to the situation and only out-qualified Prost once, when the team leader had a mechanical problem. At the end of the campaign Nelson Piquet of Brabham, on fifty-nine points, was to pip Alain Prost on fifty-seven points, among pit-lane accusations of running 'rocket fuel' in the Brazilian's tanks!

The Renault driver was to express his frustration in style. He criticised his team and its technical partner, Elf, for not giving him equipment worthy of a real chance of the title. These were strong words that were resented by the management, as they implied technical malaise. Alain Prost moved on by mutual consent to McLaren but there was eventually to be a twist in the tale at the climax of his career with matters between himself and Renault ending happily. More of that later.

USA GP, 6 June 1982 (above)

Podium, French GP, 25 July 1982 (right)

Helmets, South African GP, 15 October 1983
(left)

Alain Prost, USA GP, 5 June 1983
(right)

Alain's own perspective on 1983 is welcome: 'To this day I still consider we won. Everyone knew that the fuel used by Brabham was not legal and, from the summer onwards, the lead we had built up was steadily nibbled away. The only thing we could have done to stop that was to protest. I wanted to, but the Renault management didn't and I didn't have enough weight at the time to influence the decision. We parted company on that false note. Renault deserved the title and yet we didn't win it. It was the biggest regret of my life. I always believed that something would be missing if I didn't win the World Championship with Renault. The only consolation from that season is that both the team and myself learnt certain lessons as a result.'

'Everyone knew that the fuel used by Brabham was not legal'

Nigel Mansell and
Elio de Angelis,
February 1984

Chapter Six:
So Many Engines!

The technical staff at Renault Sport increased their workload further in 1984 when Ligier became the third team to benefit from Renault engines. Meanwhile the main team had new faces in the cockpits with the departure of Alain Prost and Eddie Cheever. They were Patrick Tambay and Derek Warwick. The Renault management were to witness a good working relationship at last but one that came as a surprise for Frenchman Tambay, who had gained much of his experience in Renault's junior formulae: 'I went to Renault after a successful year with Ferrari. I was looking forward to joining the team because I thought Alain Prost and I were going to be teammates. His decision to leave came as a disappointment but his replacement, Derek Warwick, proved to be a great teammate too, someone I will always remember as being straight, frank, and honest. He was the best I had since Villeneuve. In short he became a good friend.'

Warwick's determination was obvious from the first days of his Formula One career in 1981. The Toleman taught him a lot about turbocharged engines. After three difficult seasons with that team the Briton willingly accepted Gerard Larousse's invitation. Despite being quick and brave, Derek never realised the returns for Renault that he desired. A highlight, however, was finishing second at Brands Hatch in his initial season with the French team. This meant he could bask in the popularity he enjoyed not only at home but abroad. By coincidence Patrick Tambay put in his best performance for Renault in the 1984 French Grand Prix when he too finished second.

A third driver was employed by the works Renault team at the 1984 Portuguese Grand Prix. This was young Frenchman Philippe Streiff. He teamed up with Warwick and Tambay for that weekend before being given opportunities with Renault-powered teams Ligier and especially Tyrrell in the following season. That was the 1985 season which is remembered as something of a record one at Renault Sport as no fewer than four teams raced with Renault power, Tyrrell being the newcomer.

The production manager at Renault Sport was Jean-Francois Robin: 'Despite what may generally be thought, the fact that we supplied four teams did not constitute all that big a workload for us. It simply meant producing some sixty power units at the start of the year. A single team goes through that many in the course of a season today.'

Derek Warwick, French GP, 20 May 1984 *(above)*

Andrea de Cesaris, Ligier-Renault, French GP, 20 May 1984 *(right)*

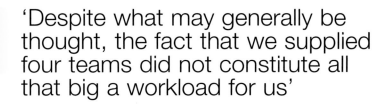

'Despite what may generally be thought, the fact that we supplied four teams did not constitute all that big a workload for us'

Patrick Tambay, French GP, 20 May 1984

With Tambay and Warwick retained, there was still an unusual opportunity afforded to Francois Henault. He had enjoyed extensive Renault Sport experience in his career and was now chosen to drive a third works Renault in the German Grand Prix at the Nürburgring. This car was significant because it featured an on-board camera, the first time one had been fitted for the full length of a Grand Prix.

At the end of the 1985 season Renault took the decision to concentrate solely on building engines and not race, until further notice, as a team. By 1986 they had withdrawn without having won the world titles, despite a number of near misses. Ironically, Alain Prost won the drivers' title again for McLaren. Bernard Dudot, now the technical director of Renault Sport explained: 'From the outset of the season, everyone had guessed that Renault's withdrawal was imminent. The financial problems were the main cause. Renault as a team had already disappeared by the end of the previous year and we were now purely engine suppliers. Our efforts essentially concentrated on Lotus and Ayrton Senna in whom we saw a potential World Champion. With eight pole positions and two wins to his name at the end of the year, he lived every bit up to his promise even if he finished no higher than fourth in the overall rankings.'

Dudot was already looking to the future. Initially unaware of this was Jean-Marie Balestre, the president of the sport's governing body, who represented the Federation du Sport Automobile of France. He was outspoken in his views of a major engine manufacturer – and a French one at that – pulling out of Formula One. However, a new perspective developed when he was informed that Renault would operate a technical surveillance unit to monitor Formula One trends: 'To have withdrawn completely would have been an unbelievable error and would have wasted irreplaceable resources, both technical and human. The foresight of Patrick Faure in setting up a technical surveillance unit will help preserve the company's expertise at the pinnacle of motor sport.'

Time would prove those words to be prophetic.

**Philippe Streiff, Portuguese GP,
21 October 1984**

Tyrrell-Renault, German GP,
4 August 1985

Bernard Dudot

Tyrell-Renault, Belgian GP, 15 September 1985

Chapter Seven:
Back to the Front

After two years' absence, Renault was back in Formula One in 1989 as engine supplier to Williams. Within six races Thierry Boutsen scored the first win for the Franco-British team in Canada. His car was powered by a latest-generation French V10. The working group, which had continued to develop the new engine under the supervision of Bernard Dudot, succeeded in their gamble and Williams-Renault finished second in the Constructors' World Championship behind McLaren-Honda. Raymond H. Levy, the chairman and CEO of Renault at the time explained to an attentive sporting world: 'We had not thrown in the towel in 1986, we had only suspended our participation in Formula One. The moment our financial difficulties looked as though they were sorting themselves out we decided to return to Formula One. We had to. Throughout its history Renault has always been at the peak of motor sport. It's part of the firm's temperament. We would only have been compromising our future if we tried to break with the traditions of the past. It was no longer a case of us building our own car, however. Our role as an engine supplier would enable us to demonstrate our expertise quite sufficiently. It did not take long for the talent and determination of Renault's staff to prove itself. Thanks to the working group which had been maintained under the leadership of Bernard Dudot, we reaped top results immediately.'

The seeds of the fruitful alliance with Williams had been planted many years before by Bernard Casin. He had been appointed Head of Renault Sport in 1985 at the beginning of its most turbulent period. In the early 1970s Casin had been an after-sales director in South Africa for Renault and it was at Kylami that he met Frank Williams for the first time. As Lotus, Ligier and Tyrrell moved on from Renault, Casin still kept focused on Formula One developments. When the decision to return was made, Casin revitalised that contact with Frank Williams. They met to progress and conclude a partnership agreement. This link was to have an impact on the sport for many years to come.

Frank Williams,
Portuguese GP,
26 September 1993
(left)

Podium, Canadian
GP, 17 June 1989
(right)

'We had not thrown in the towel in 1986, we had only suspended our participation in Formula One'

RENAULT F1
Beyond the Yellow Teapot

Behind the scenes the long-term contribution of Bernard Dudot was coming to the fore. He had worked for Renault-Alpine and had a full-time post from 1968. There was eventually a major role on the development of the turbocharged engines for Renault's Formula One campaign. When Renault stopped the chassis and engine programme before the 1986 season, and the engine supply within a year, it fell to Dudot to launch Renault Sport's technical surveillance and keep the staff on-side. A new programme eventually emerged around the naturally aspirated V10 which saw a golden era unfold in the 1990s.

As that decade opened, the drivers on the Williams-Renault team continued to put in top performances as parts of the puzzle were gradually put into place. Thierry Boutsen recalls being 'punch drunk as a result of testing': 'I have never driven so much in so short a lapse of time! We clocked thousands of kilometres during private testing both before and during the season. We never stopped. It was like forced labour! Yet the car still wasn't quick enough and we were going through a lot of tyres. That in turn meant we had to stop to change rubber in the course of certain races compared with one change for the others. The 1990 season also saw qualifying fuels make an appearance for the first time and Elf had introduced some fantastic products ideally suited to the characteristics of our engine. During qualifying we could rev higher and the car behaved as it was 60kg lighter. The engine itself evolved considerably between the start and the end of the season. I think we must have gained something in the order of a second per lap.' By the end of the racing calendar Boutsen had won the Hungarian Grand Prix, finished second at the British Grand Prix and third in the USA. Teammate Ricardo Patrese claimed a victory at the San Marino Grand Prix.

Onwards and upwards!

Thierry Boutsen, January 1989 *(above)*

Renault Sport assembly workshop, January 1989 *(left)*

Chapter Eight:
The Prize in Sight

By 1991 **Williams** and Renault were practically at the summit of their art. The duel that saw Boutsen's replacement, Nigel Mansell, take on McLaren's Ayrton Senna only turned in favour of the Brazilian towards the end of the year. Within the Williams-Renault team was a belief that it was only a matter of time. The battle the following season would be even fiercer, with Williams-Renault a technical length ahead.

Christian Contzen was managing director of Renault at that time: 'We were so very close to winning the title in 1991. However, we shouldn't harbour any regrets. Our relative failure taught us that to be champion you had to be perfect. We had nearly been perfect. Nearly too perfect. The Williams chassis boasted a host of innovative features, which the others were already looking to copy, and the potential of the V10 engine was extremely high. At Viry-Chatillon, Bernard Dudot and his team had put in some remarkable work and ours were among the best engines available. On top of that Nigel Mansell demonstrated his exceptional talent. We had been given a lesson in humility. We have since continued our quest for total quality and performance through perfection.'

Contzen's praise of Mansell was interesting in light of the Briton's long haul to the top. He had been promoted from test driver to team member at Lotus as far back as 1980. By 1983 he was enjoying Renault power with the V6 turbo. However, he never won a race at Lotus and in 1985 began his on-off relationship with Williams. In his seventy-second race he won the British Grand Prix at Brands Hatch. Mansell became a contender for the world title in 1986 and 1987. He joined Ferrari in 1989 for two seasons before returning to Williams in 1991.

So began a new dawn for Mansell at the wheel of the Renault naturally aspirated V10. 1992 was the year for both parties to climb to the summit of the sport. Fifteen years after the debut of the 'Yellow Teapot', Renault and Mansell succeeded in winning the title that had proved so elusive to both. In fact it was a doubly successful campaign with both the Drivers' and Constructors'

World Championships. Nigel set a new record at the time for his nine victories and fourteen pole positions. He secured the crown at the Hungarian Grand Prix in August.

Mansell and Patrese, German GP, 28 July 1991

'Our relative failure taught us that to be champion you had to be perfect'

Nigel Mansell, Canadian GP,
2 June 1991

Patrick Faure, the president of Renault Sport and executive vice-president of sales and marketing was more than pleased: 'At last we had achieved the objectives we had set ourselves. Our aim in 1989 was to win one, if possible, two titles. That we have done. In doing so we have proved that Renault is among the best, if not the best, manufacturers of engines in the world. I would like to dedicate this victory to all whose individual contributions since 1977 have allowed Renault to make it to the summit of Formula One. It is our ongoing commitment which has won the day. We took a big risk in terms of Renault's image and we have learnt a great deal.'

There was a strange twist in the tale, for Mansell and Williams parted company again. Terms could not be agreed for the following season and Nigel Mansell left to contest the Champ Car series in America, winning the championship in his 'rookie' year! So the World Champion's departure allowed destiny to play a further hand as Alain Prost was to be his replacement.

**South African GP,
1 March 1992**
(above)

**Podium, Mexican
GP, 22 March 1992**
(right)

'Our aim in 1989 was to win one, if possible, two titles. That we have done. In doing so we have proved that Renault is among the best, if not the best, manufacturers of engines in the world'

French GP, 4 July 1993

Chapter Nine:
The Confirmation

The **Williams-Renault team** won the Drivers' and Constructors' titles for the second consecutive year. 1993 therefore confirmed the success of the previous year. For the first time – and at the French Grand Prix – four Renault engines started the race on the first and second lines of the grid. Damon Hill and Alain Prost in their Williams-Renaults, Martin Brundle and Mark Blundell in their Ligier-Renaults.

While the acquisition of Alain Prost made the headlines, the promotion of Damon Hill from test driver was more low key. Hill had been with Williams as a test driver since 1991 and had taken race opportunities in 1992 with a Brabham team then at the wrong end of the grid. His first podium finish for Williams-Renault came at the Brazilian Grand Prix as runner-up. The seeds were planted for an upwardly mobile career, which would see him eventually emulate the success of his father Graham in becoming World Champion. However, in 1993, the focus of attention was understandably on Damon's famous team partner.

With three World titles and a handsome number of victories under his belt, Prost could have stayed in retirement. However, the fact that he had never achieved his ambition with Renault gnawed at him. After a season away from the circuits the Frenchman signed for Williams-Renault. When he recorded his fourth World title Alain Prost decided the time was right to finally bring his illustrious career to a close: 'Everything went perfectly well in the Williams-Renault team this year. Another season together and I think we would have had a great time all round. Considering the relationship I have developed in the team, the potential of the Renault engine and the effects of the new regulations on the chassis, it would have been much better next year. But no matter, my mind is made up. It wasn't an easy decision but I will stick to it. I am very happy to end my career with this fourth title. I've gone full circle. Together we've succeeded in doing what I had hoped for with all my might since 1983 – to be World Champion with Renault.'

Alain Prost, 1993

'Together we've succeeded in doing what I had hoped for with all my might since 1983 – to be World Champion with Renault'

French GP, 4 July 1993

Bernard Dudot, Patrick Faure and Christian Contzen, Belgian GP, 29 August 1993

Chapter Ten:
Through a Veil of Tears

A secretive close-season deal brought another World Champion into the ranks of Williams-Renault, one who had enjoyed the use of Renault engines in his quick rise through the ranks. Having an engine deal with Renault had allowed Lotus to persuade Ayrton Senna to join their team for the 1985 season. Senna developed a strong working relationship with technical director Gerard Larousse and for three seasons they were to achieve much for Team Lotus.

In 1985, at the Portuguese Grand Prix, Senna earned the first of the sixty-five pole positions of his career. His Lotus-Renault led all the way and he also set the fastest lap to gain the 'triple whammy'. For two years the Brazilian made full use of his Renault engine to record a series of brilliant drives before moving to McLaren to reach the pinnacle of World titles in competition with Alain Prost. When he came to Williams-Renault in 1994 he wanted to emulate the Frenchman and gain a fourth World title. Like Prost he also wanted to complete the circle. Williams had given him his first Formula One test drive at Donington Park in 1983. Of course, he had the extra dimension of teaming up again with Renault who had helped elevate him to a competitive level in the sport. Sentiment aside, Ayrton Senna also knew he was inheriting a competitive racing package. The prospects were very bright until 1 May at Imola and tragedy.

Patrick Faure, president of Renault Sport, had a difficult decision to make: 'Ayrton Senna's disappearance was a tragic loss, which shook Renault Sport and the whole of the company deeply and indeed continues to move us today. Nevertheless, very quickly, we took the decision to maintain our presence at the highest level of motor sport by setting ourselves the target of winning the 1994 Constructors' World Championship. It seemed the best homage we could pay Ayrton Senna, rather than pulling out of Formula One, was, on the contrary, to keep on fighting. And fighting to win. We were by no means certain we would succeed, but circumstances have proved that we were right. You do not win if you do not set ambitious targets.'

**Ayrton Senna,
French GP,
7 July 1985**

'It seemed the best homage we could pay Ayrton Senna, rather than pulling out of Formula One, was, on the contrary, to keep on fighting. And fighting to win'

Team portraits, January 1994

Meanwhile, Senna's fatal accident had thrust the understated Damon Hill into the role of team leader and the young test driver David Coulthard into Senna's seat. Encouragingly, Hill had a hattrick of victories to his credit in 1993 at Hungary, Belgium and Italy. He had been teammate to two great World Champions as well as being the son of a double World Champion. Eventually he won six Grand Prix in 1994 but failed to take the title after a controversial collision with Michael Schumacher during the final race of the season at Adelaide, Australia.

Coulthard took his opportunity and his first podium position was a second place at the Portuguese Grand Prix. However, the Williams management did not provide him with a full schedule of races in his debut season and replaced him for four Grand Prix with Nigel Mansell. The former champion commuted across the Atlantic for a third spell with the team. In typical swashbuckling style he won the final race of the season, and his Williams career, in Australia.

For the company it was the third consecutive year that Renault had proved itself the best engine manufacturer in the world. Now it was poised for a fresh challenge in 1995 when a new association with Benetton was announced.

Damon Hill,
Monaco GP,
15 May 1994 (above)

Ayrton Senna,
March 1994 (below)

Damon Hill, British GP, 10 July 1994

Benetton-Renault, Monaco GP, 28 May 1995

Chapter Eleven:
Success Assured

When the Benetton family invited the head of marketing in the American fashion market to put their racing team in order, the move surprised many. Flavio Briatore had no motor sport background. However, he displayed great insight with his first move. This was to secure the services of a young German driver, Michael Schumacher. To many motor racing pundits the emergence of Schumacher confounded belief. He had been a journeyman from his karting days as a child to being one of a crop of drivers in the Mercedes junior team. Given a very impressive first drive by Jordan at Spa towards the end of the 1991 season, he was snapped up by Benetton and became World Champion in only his third full season in 1994. That was a factor in persuading Renault to commit to Benetton from 1995. Briatore's proposition was simple: 'I've got the best driver. You give me the best engine!'

The eventual result was summed up succinctly by Benetton Formula One's managing director: 'The first year of partnership has been a very successful year for Benetton and Renault. The double victory of both Drivers' and Constructors' World Championshiphas been pursued all season and achieved through the hard work of both Renault and Benetton. With Benetton this season Renault has added significant new records: their first win at the Monaco GP and their first pole position at the Canadian GP. These achievements, along with the others of the 1995 season, are a confirmation of the value of this partnership.'

Williams as well as Benetton benefited from the new RS7 engine. It won sixteen out of the seventeen Grand Prix races, eleven with Benetton and five with Williams. In five races the Renault engine took first and second places, and in three races it took the first three places. The RS7 claimed sixteen pole positions, of which four were with Benetton and twelve with Williams. It also set fourteen lap records, eight with Benetton and six with Williams.

So the season was an overwhelming triumph, with four Renault drivers taking the first four championship places. In winning his

Flavio Briatore
and Michael
Schumacher, Pacific
GP, 22 October 1995

To many motor racing pundits the emergence of Schumacher confounded belief

Benetton-Renault, Brazilian GP, 26 March 1995

Williams-Renault, Canadian GP,
11 June 1995

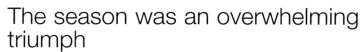

second title, Schumacher got the better of Hill again. Damon was not dispirited and relished the next phase of their encounter, although his German rival had moved to Ferrari by 1996. However, many felt that Williams didn't really appreciate David Coulthard's potential. This may have been the reason he moved to McLaren, with whom he was to enjoy a sustained career.

The season was an overwhelming triumph

**Benetton-Renault, Monaco GP,
28 May 1995**

Williams-Renault,
French GP, 2 July 1995

Chapter Twelve:
Williams to the Fore

For the 1996 Formula One season, Renault again supplied engines to two teams: Williams, who introduced Canadian Jacques Villeneuve to partner Damon Hill, and Benetton, with Austrian driver Gerhard Berger and Frenchman Jean Alesi. The engine in question was the RS8, a new version of the renowned V10. It was with this engine that Renault produced the amazing Formula One feat of Hill, Villeneuve, Alesi and Berger taking the first four places in the French Grand Prix.

At Williams, Villeneuve announced his entry into Formula One with a pole position on his debut at Melbourne, Australia. In the race itself, Hill had to use all his experience to keep Villeneuve from an initial victory. This inevitably arrived in his fourth outing at the Nürburgring for the European GP. This meant the Englishman knew he had to find new depths of achievement and was under pressure from his teammate all the way to the final race. Victory in Japan finally gave Hill the title.

Frank Williams was certainly a satisfied man at the end of the season: 'The Williams-Renault partnership has grown in strength year on year and the results achieved in 1996 are testimony to that strength. We pride ourselves in having achieved these results as a team. The commitment of each company to another is exceptional. It is a partnership of which we are very proud. Although achieving records is not necessarily the main target, we truly hope that together we can deliver exciting, competitive and championship-winning motor sport again in 1997, ensuring that Renault's present chapter within Formula One closes on a high.'

With Damon Hill finding himself in the same situation as Nigel Mansell in 1993 – a British World Champion with no seat at Williams for the subsequent season – he took a radical move towards the back of the grid with Arrows. Jacques Villeneuve moved to team leader and was supported by Heinz-Harald Frentzen. The title was fought between Jacques Villeneuve and Michael Schumacher across the whole season, with victory secured by Villeneuve in the final race at Jerez, Spain – a brilliant finish to a season that

Damon Hill,
Japanese GP,
13 October 1996

Jacques Villeneuve,
European GP, 28 April 1996

Jacques Villeneuve,
Australian GP, 10 March 1996

Benetton-Renault, Monaco
GP, 11 May 1997

included seven victories and ten pole positions. Villeneuve and Williams thus added to Renault's collection of World titles to coincide with the company taking a break from the sport.

After innovating as the first manufacturer to develop a turbocharged engine for Formula One racing, Renault came back as the first manufacturer to put a V10 in an Formula One chassis. This time it produced six Constructors' World Championships in a row and five Drivers' World titles.

During their association Renault and Williams proved their technical prowess. Frank Williams, since knighted, has always looked at the decision to overcome any potential difficulties in an Anglo-French alliance as one of the best of his lifetime. The working relationship was always based on genuine mutual respect: 'The men from Renault have always viewed me as more than just a man in a wheelchair.' Sir Frank was paralysed in a road accident in 1986. He recovered from that major personal setback to take the Williams team – with the input of Renault – to the heights of the sport.

'The Williams-Renault partnership has grown in strength year on year and the results achieved in 1996 are testimony to that strength'

Williams-Renault, Canadian GP, 26 June 1996.

Jaques Villeneuve, British GP,
13 July 1997. Another victory
en route to his world title

RENAULT F1 1977 - 1997
Beyond the Yellow Teapot

**Group photo,
European GP,
26 October 1997**
(right)

**Podium, European
GP, 26 October
1997** *(opposite)*

Epilogue: **Back On Course**

Between 1998 and 2000, the company's most recent transitional period, Williams and Arrows were powered by Renault-designed engines that were re-badged as Mecachrome and, later, Supertec. It was Christian Contzen who kept Renault Sport's foot in the door through these initiatives and a handful of customer teams. He again established a technical surveillance team that could produce a new engine featuring the latest technology. It was Contzen back in 1995 who opted to run two competitive teams with Williams and Benetton. This allowed extra technical data that put Renault at the head of the pack. Now, after a working lifetime with the parent company, Christian Contzen was at the forefront of Renault's Formula One return when Benetton was taken over by Renault as the new millennium dawned.

Another veteran who had a perspective on Renault's racing history and was delighted with the return was Pierre Dupasquier, Michelin's motor sport director. He had worked with Jean-Pierre Jabouille on Renault's breakthrough success at Dijon in 1979. Over the subsequent years the technical partnership between Renault and Michelin was excellent, progressive and proven on track.

Finally, the greatest perspective could belong to the motor sport director of fuel company Elf, Francois Guiter. In the 1970s he arranged the finance for a feasibility study into a high-performance engine. This set in motion the development of the turbocharged engine that has had such an impact on this story. It was he who persuaded Renault's engineers that, one day, a turbocharged French engine should be a competitive force in Formula One. Guiter also conducted a survey to establish that Formula One was a potent marketing tool for a major manufacturer.

Both parties built an association dating back to 1970 to commit themselves to the cause. Although Renault has taken a break from Formula One on several occasions, Elf has also had a policy of maintaining a small technical unit to monitor trends. So in 2001 the affinity partners were poised. They were delighted with the feedback from Giancarlo Fisichella at Spa, Belgium when he confirmed the team was back on course. By finishing third the Italian scored the first podium finish for the latest-generation Renault V10 engine, which rival teams considered revolutionary. Now where had that been stated before?

USA GP, 1 October 1978

Canadian GP, 8 October 1978

Movers and Shakers

BERNARD DUDOT

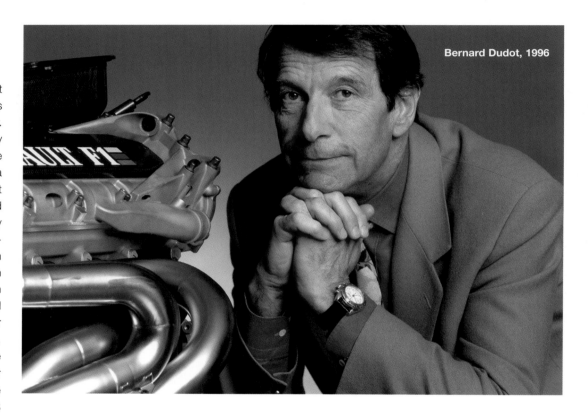

Bernard Dudot, 1996

Bernard combined his interest in motor sport with his studies at the renowned Centre D'Etudes Superieres de Techniques Industrielles in Nancy. He sought employment with the Alpine company upon graduation in the late 1960s. This gave him the opportunity to work on the design of a Formula Three engine. This was the path that would lead Alpine to work with Renault and lead to Grand Prix racing within a decade. Significantly he worked closely in Formula Three with Jean-Pierre Jabouille and they enjoyed success on track. Bernard moved to work at Viry-Chatillon in 1973 and was seconded to America to research turbocharging. Upon his return in 1975 he worked on developing a turbocharged V6 2-litre engine for Renault's involvement in the Le Mans 24-Hours. In secret Dudot was also developing a 1.5-litre turbocharged engine for an impending move for Renault into Formula One. All was revealed at the Michelin test track at Clermont-Ferrand in 1976 when Jabouilee and Dudot continued their working relationship, ready for the ultimate challenge. The track debut was at the British Grand Prix in 1977 and, as recorded elsewhere in depth in this history, Jabouille opened the account for Renault with victory in the French Grand Prix at Dijon-Prenois in 1979.

In 1980 Bernard Dudot was made technical director of Renault Sport. Once Renault had ceased its combined chassis and engine operation in 1985 and decided to wind down its supply to other teams by 1986, it fell to the Frenchman to show his skills of leadership and power of personality by keeping his engineers onside. With the support of Patrick Faure he introduced a technical surveillance programme. The task was then met of producing a naturally aspirated V10, which succeeded in winning six Constructors' World Championship titles between 1992 and 1997.

Bernard had an interesting choice to make at the conclusion of this campaign when Renault decided to opt out of Formula One again. Alain Prost, with whom he had worked in two phases of the legendary racer's career, offered Bernard the role of technical director at Prost Grand Prix. This he accepted and held for a season-and-a-half in a struggling team. Once replaced, he crossed the Atlantic to work in the Indy Racing League. Eventually he returned to his spiritual home with the happy conclusion of being appointed as manager of Renault Sport in 2003.

**Dudot, Schweitzer, Robin, Faure
and Contzen, June 1996**

Patrick Faure with the World
Championship trophy, February 1996

PATRICK FAURE

The son of a French cabinet minister, Patrick graduated from the elite business school Ecole Nationale d'Adminstration. He did not enter the commercial world at first and was a civil servant. However, his management skills with a precision engineering firm led to his being offered a role with Renault. He specialised in sales and was eventually made head of Renault in Britain in the early 1980s. He was promoted to the board of directors of the company in 1986 and given responsibility for Renault Sport. This coincided with a difficult time for the company. He had to make a balanced decision over the future of Renault in Formula One. He decided to withdraw the team partly because the turbo engines were being phased out with designs in place for a new normally aspirated engine. Bernard Dudot was charged with the task of research and development ready for the time being right for Renault's return to the circuits. Dudot designed the Renault V10 and Renault returned to the fold to be the sport's dominant force of the 1990s.

Patrick remains as president of Renault Sport and has overseen yet another dormant period and successful return to Grand Prix racing in the new century.

JEAN-JACQUES HIS

Jean-Jacques joined Renault immediately after graduating from the prestigious engineering college Ecole Centrale des Arts et Manufactures in Paris in 1972. He was not involved in motor sport and specialised in diesel engines. In 1981 he was given a senior role at the parent company in the research and development department. By 1984 Bernard Dudot needed a candidate for a similar role at Renault Sport and His was invited to move across to Viry-Chatillon. The withdrawal of Renault from Formula One in the mid-eighties saw Enzo Ferrari swoop for Jean-Jacques His. This gave the Frenchman a fascinating and educative period as manager of the competition engine department at the Italian team headquarters. At Marenello he

Jean-Jacques His, 1996

Flavio Briatore, Belgian GP, 27 August 1995

supervised the various racing projects including the Ferrari V6 turbo and a 3.5-litre V12.

However, once Renault was able to return to the Grand Prix circuits it did not take Bernard Dudot long to contact Jean-Jacques and convince him to return home. His input was an obvious factor in the continued success of Williams and Benetton in the 1990s. When Formula One was wound down again he moved back into the automobile division as head of engine design for Renault. When the call came for Renault's Formula One return in the new millennium, His was pleased to renew old acquaintances as technical director and later

managing director of Renault Sport. However, he was replaced by Flavio Briatore before the 2003 season. He moved to a division of Ferrari soon afterwards but his contribution to Renault Formula One will always be recognised.

FLAVIO BRIATORE

Flavio Briatore did not emerge from a motor racing background and discovered the sport when the Benetton family asked him to organise their Formula One team on a sound financial basis. He had previously been in charge of the Benetton Group's fashion retail operation in America.

He decided on a 'root and branch' overhaul that impacted on all aspects including the factory, the pit garage, the marketing and, of course, the personnel. This efficiency drive in place, he then recruited top talent such as Michael Schumacher in the cockpit and Tom Walkinshaw in the workshop. This combination saw a successful but controversial 1994 World Championship for Benetton-Ford and a continuation on the peak for Benetton-Renault in 1995. When Schumacher was lured to Ferrari he was accompanied in his move by a coterie of top Benetton engineers. The team then found it hard to stay at the very top in the following seasons. Briatore was dropped by Benetton and organised a deal to purchase old Renault engines and rebrand them as Supertec. He returned to management with Benetton when Renault acquired the team in 2000 and became managing director of Renault Sport in 2003. He is regarded as one of the sport's most colourful characters with as much copy produced about him in the gossip columns as on the sports pages!

Christian Contzen, British GP, 13 July 1997

CHRISTIAN CONTZEN

Christian Contzen was managing director of Renault Sport from 1991 to 2002. A Belgian, he joined the parent company as an after-sales representative in Brussels in 1960. A solid career over the next quarter-century, mainly in sales, saw him take a series of major regional positions until being appointed marketing director of Renault in 1987.

His move to Renault Sport meant a strong working relationship with Williams during a very successful period. He was a particular admirer of Nigel Mansell, who achieved the Drivers' World Championship in 1992. The Briton's flair and courage was as much appreciated behind the scenes as it was among the fans and the media.

Despite the tie-up with Williams, it was Contzen's correct decision to supply a second team in Benetton and draw additional technical information, which enhanced the company's operation. When Renault withdrew from Formula One at the conclusion of Jacques Villeneuve's title-winning season in 1997, Christian Contzen reinforced the policy of maintaining a technical surveillance team at Viry-Chatillon and also engaged a small team of engineers to continue with engine development. This assisted the return of Renault to the sport in 2000.

Renault Drivers' Career and Race Record

JEAN-PIERRE JABOUILLE

Born 1 October 1942, Paris, France

Jean-Pierre Jabouille,
Austrian GP,
13 August 1978

Jean-Pierre first competed at the Mont Dore hill climb in 1965, driving his own Alpine Renault. The next year he competed in the new Renault 8 Gordini series and was the wheel of a Mini-Marcos in 1,000km races in France and Italy.

By 1967 he had acquired a Formula Three Brabham and, with the assistance of his mechanic – one Jacques Lafitte – began to progress in the French Formula Three series. After two successful seasons he was hired by the Alpine Renault team for the 1969 campaign. His performances caught the eye of Matra and they offered a contract which kept him busy in both Formula Two and sports car racing.

His actual Formula One debut was with Tyrrell at Paul Ricard for the 1975 French Grand Prix but for the main part his diary revolved around the European Formula Two Championship, which he won in 1976 with an Elf 2 chassis. He was already involved with Renault's Formula One aspirations and secret tests. However, he initially had to bear the brunt of much mirth when, from 1977, the new Renault turbo chugged its merry way around the Grand Prix circuits. However, by 1979 the joke was on his tormentors with his historic victory at the French Grand Prix around Dijon-Prenois. That highlight was repeated again in 1980 at the Austrian Grand Prix around the Osterreichring. Sadly, he received serious leg injuries at the Canadian Grand Prix that season.

He was offered a place at Ligier in 1981 but was still suffering problems with his legs, After failing to qualify at Monaco he took the decision to retire and take a management role with the team. By 1984 the lure of action was too strong and Jean-Pierre joined Peugeot to compete in the French Touring Car Championship. In 1992 and 1993 he was a member of the Peugeot team at Le Mans. On finally retiring as a driver he was appointed as Head of Peugeot Sport and its Formula One programme.

45 GRAND PRIX FOR RENAULT:

1977
Great Britain: Did not finish
Holland: Did not finish
Italy: Did not finish
United States East: Did not finish

1978
South Africa: Did not finish
United States West: Did not finish
Monaco: 10th
Belgium: Not classified
Spain: 13th
Sweden: Did not finish
France: Did not finish
Great Britain: Did not finish
Germany: Did not finish
Austria: Did not finish

Holland: Did not finish
Italy: Did not finish
United States East: 4th
Cananda: 12th

1979
Argentina: Did not finish
Brazil: 10th
South Africa: Did not finish
Spain: Did not finish
Belgium: Did not finish
Monaco: 8th
France: 1st
Great Britain: Did not finish
Germany: Did not finish
Austria: Did not finish
Holland: Did not finish
Italy: 14th
Canada: Did not finish

United States East: Did not finish

1980
Argentina: Did not finish
Brazil: Did not finish
South Africa: Did not finish
United States West: 10th
Belgium: Did not finish
Monaco: Did not finish
France: Did not finish
Great Britain: Did not finish
Germany: Did not finish
Austria: 1st
Holland: Did not finish
Italy: Did not finish
Canada: Accident

RENE ARNOUX

Born 4 July 1948, Grenoble, France

Rene was successful in various Renault-supported categories of the French motor sport scene before coming to prominence as a Grand Prix driver. He won the Formula Super Renault Championship in 1975 and the European Formula Two Championship in 1977. This obvious talent gained him a place with the factory Renault turbo team from 1979 to 1982. With eighteen pole positions, the most by a driver not to gain a world title, Arnoux was one of the fastest racers on the circuits in his Renault years. His ability to stir matters up with team partners Jabouille and Prost saw him join Ferrari in 1983. That season he won the Canadian, German and Dutch Grand Prix. He was released by his Italian bosses suddenly after the 1985 Brazilian Grand Prix and did not race again until 1986 when he was signed by Ligier-Renault, for whom he tried manfully to bring some points. He stayed with the team until the age of forty when, finding no further opportunities at that age, he moved into sports car racing. He competed at Le Mans in the 1990s and also in French ice racing.

74 GRAND PRIX FOR RENAULT AND LIGIER-RENAULT

1979 (Renault)
Argentina: Did not finish
Brazil: Did not finish
South Africa: Did not finish
Spain: 9th
Belgium: Did not finish
Monaco: Accident
France: 3rd
Great Britain: 2nd
Germany: Did not finish
Austria: 6th
Holland: Did not finish
Italy: Did not finish
Canada: Accident
United States: 2nd

1980
Argentina: Did not finish
Brazil: 1st
South Africa: 1st
United States West: 9th
Belgium: 4th
Monaco: Accident
France: 5th
Great Britain: Not classified
Germany: Did not finish
Austria: 9th
Holland: 2nd

Italy: 10th
Canada: Did not finish
United States East: 7th

1981
United States West: 8th
Brazil: Accident
Argentina; 5th
San Marino: 8th
Monaco: Accident
Spain: 9th
France: 4th
Great Britain: 9th
Germany: 13th
Austria: 2nd
Holland: Did not finish
Italy: Accident
Canada: Accident
United States: Did not finish

1982
South Africa: 3rd
Brazil: Accident
United States West: Accident
San Marino: Did not finish
Belgium: Did not finish
Monaco: Did not finish

United States East: 10th
Canada: Accident
Holland: Accident
Great Britain: Accident
France: 1st
Germany: 2nd
Austria: Did not finish
Switzerland: 16th
Italy: 1st
United States: Did not finish

1986 (Ligier-Renault)
Brazil: 4th
Spain: Did not finish
San Marino: Did not finish
Monaco: 5th
Belgium: Did not finish
Canada: 6th
United States: Accident
France: 5th
Great Britain: 4th
Germany: 4th
Hungary: Did not finish
Austria: 10th
Italy: Did not finish
Portugal: 7th
Mexico: 15th
Australia: 7th

Rene Arnoux, British GP, 14 July 1978

ALAIN PROST

Born 24 February 1955, Lorette Saint Chamond, France

Prost started in kart racing in his teens. He entered the Volant Elf competition at Paul Ricard in 1975, securing the prize of a drive in Formula Renault for 1976. He won the French Formula Renault Championship by a wide margin in that debut season, then moved to Formula Renault Europe for 1977 where he was a class above everyone in taking that title. Promoted immediately into Formula Three by Renault, he had taken both the French and European Championships by 1979. The same year, McLaren invited Alain to join them as a test driver and he was offered his Formula One debut for the 1980 season. He scored points in his first two Grand Prix but was injured in his third. Back from his broken wrist by May, he continued to get among the points. Renault moved in for him and he crossed over to his national team, leaving the lawyers very busy. Ended his first year with Renault placed fifth in the Drivers' World Championship with victories in France, Holland and Italy to his credit. He started the 1982 season with two victories in South Africa and Brazil but the team became bogged down in reliability problems as the year unfolded and he did not win again. However, Alain still finished fourth in the title chase. By 1983 the elusive title

was within sight, assisted by victories in France, Belgium, Britain and Austria. However, Prost lost out to Piquet by two points amid a controversial debate about the Brabham team fuel. McLaren took the unhappy Frenchman back and in 1984 he was pipped to the title by his accomplished team partner Niki Lauda. However, 1985 saw Prost win his first World Championship with McLaren and he doubled up in 1986 by outgunning the strong dual challenge of Nelson Piquet and Nigel Mansell at Williams-Honda. McLaren were not so competitive in 1987 and Alain finished fourth. The whole scene was revitalised in 1988 with the acquisition of Ayrton Senna as his team partner and Honda as the engine suppliers. It was the turn of Senna to pip Prost to the title. Their domination continued in 1989 but with fierce tension between them. This culminated in Prost gaining his third title in controversial circumstances after driving into Senna in the decider at Suzuka. Time to move on (!) and so Ferrari was the next port of call in 1990. He won five races and revived their fortunes but not his own as Senna returned the compliment of the previous year by winning the title at the Japanese Grand Prix by driving the Frenchman off the circuit.

Ferrari suffered much internal strife in 1991 and Prost was not slow to criticise them through the media. He was fired and decided to take a sabbatical. He was pleased to team up with Williams-Renault for 1993 and finish his career with a fourth World Championship and seven victories flying the flag for his home engine manufacturer. He was signed as a 'special ambassador' for Renault and eventually as a consultant for McLaren-Mercedes. By 1997 he had convinced Peugeot to back his bid to take over Ligier with a future engine deal for 1998 until 2000. A strong base seemed in place already with Olivier Panis as his number one driver and deals with Mugen-Honda engines and Bridgestone tyres. The JS45 proved competitive but it was still not an easy season. The Peugeot years proved unfortunately to be unsuccessful. The car was very unreliable and the Prost-Peugeot relationship broke down in acrimony by 2000. The great driver could not match his success when he moved to team owner and his Formula One days ended with his having to sell much of his shareholding before the team eventually went out of business in 2002.

Alain Prost, Argentinian GP, 12 April 1981

62 GRAND PRIX FOR RENAULT AND WILLIAMS-RENAULT:

1981 (Renault)
United States West: Accident
Brazil: Accident
Argentina: 3rd
San Marino: Did not finish
Belgium: Did not finish
Monaco: Did not finish
Spain: Accident
France: 1st
Great Britain: Did not finish
Germany: 2nd
Austria: Did not finish
Holland: 1st
Italy: 1st
Canada: Accident
United States East: 2nd

1982
South Africa; 1st
Brazil: 1st
United States West: Accident
San Marino: Did not finish
Belgium: Accident

Monaco: 7th
United States East: Not classified
Canada: Did not finish
Holland: Did not finish
Great Britain: 6th
France: 2nd
Germany: Did not finish
Austria: 8th
Switzerland: 2nd
Italy: Did not finish
United States West: 4th

1983
Brazil: 7th
United States West: 11th
France: 1st
San Marino: 2nd
Monaco: 3rd
Belgium: 1st
United States East: 8th
Canada: 5th
Great Britain: 1st
Germany: 4th

Austria: 1st
Holland; Accident
Italy: Did not finish
Europe: 2nd
South Africa: Did not finish

1993 (Williams-Renault)
South Africa: 1st
Brazil: Accident
Europe: 3rd
San Marino: 1st
Spain: 1st
Monaco: 4th
Canada: 1st
France: 1st
Great Britain: 1st
Germany: 1st
Hungary: 12th
Belgium: 3rd
Italy: 12th
Portugal: 2nd
Japan: 2nd
Australia: 2nd

**Eddie Cheever, Brazilian GP,
13 March 1983**

EDDIE CHEEVER

Born 10 January 1958, Phoenix, Arizona, USA

Eddie spent his formative years in Italy and was a competitive kart racer. He made his Formula One debut at the 1978 South African GP with Hesketh while still a Formula Two driver with Osella. When that team entered Formula One in 1980 Eddie moved up with them. He then had a series of other teams in successive seasons, spending 1981 with Tyrrell and 1982 with Ligier before becoming Alain Prost's team partner at Renault in 1983. He was in the shadow of the illustrious Frenchman but did get on the rostrum with third places in France, Belgium and Italy plus a second place in Canada.

Cheever moved on again in 1984 to Alfa Romeo, actually staying for a second season. Arrows was his final team and the American was with them from 1986 to 1989.

He decided to move back to his home country and enjoyed a successful career in the Indy Car series, culminating in winning the Indy 500 in 1998. More recently, he was a team owner in the Indy Racing League.

15 GRAND PRIX FOR RENAULT:

1983
Brazil: Did not finish
United States West: did not finish
France: 3rd
San Marino: Did not finish
Monaco: Did not finish
Belgium: 3rd
United States East: Did not finish

Canada: 2nd
Great Britain: Did not finish
Germany: Did not finish
Austria: 4th
Holland: Did not finish
Italy: 3rd
Europe: 10th
South Africa 6th

PATRICK TAMBAY

Born 25 June 1949, Paris, France

Patrick joined McLaren in 1978 when they were by no means the force of previous seasons. He was with them for two years before moving to Ligier. After the death of Gilles Villeneuve in 1982, Ferrari offered the vacant seat to the popular Frenchman. He enjoyed victories for the Italian team over two seasons but in 1984 found himself without a place and was snapped up by Renault. Patrick particularly enjoyed achieving second place in his home GP in 1984 but he had only two other rostrum spots for Renault, coming third at Portugal and San Marino in 1985. He retired from the Formula One scene after a frustrating season with the Lola team in 1986 and moved into other forms of motor sport. Patrick drove for Jaguar in sports car racing while also competing in the famous Paris-Dakar desert race. He twice finished in the top three in the latter. He was a major shareholder in Larousse Formula One in the mid-1990s and an adviser to the team. Now actively involved in television commentary on motor sport in France.

30 GRAND PRIX FOR RENAULT:

1984
Brazil: 6th
South Africa: Did not finish
Belgium: 8th
San Marino; Accident
France: 2nd
Monaco: Accident
United States East: Did not finish
United States West: Accident
Great Britain: 8th

Germany: 5th
Austria: Did not finish
Holland: 6th
Italy: Did not finish
Europe: Did not finish
Portugal: 7th

1985
Brazil: 5th
Portugal: 3rd
San Marino: 3rd
Monaco: Accident

Canada: 7th
United States East: Accident
France: 6th
Great Britain: Accident
Germany: Accident
Austria: 10th
Holland: Did not finish
Italy: 7th
Belgium: Did not finish
Europe: 12th
Australia: Did not finish

**Patrick Tambay,
December 1983**

Derek Warwick,
Monaco GP,
3 June 1984

DEREK WARWICK

Born 27 August 1954, Alresford, Hampshire, England

The battling Brit came into Formula One in 1981 from oval-circuit stock car racing in the UK. Derek's first team was Toleman and they consistently failed to qualify in their first season together. Performances improved for both parties as the seasons unfolded, which led to an offer from Renault to replace Alain Prost in 1984. Unfortunately this was not the most competitive period in Renault's history and results were hard to maintain.

Warwick's best results were two second places in the Belgian and British Grand Prix of his first season with his French bosses. Lack of results meant moves to other teams with challenges such as Brabham and Arrows in the late 1980s. Derek turned his attention to sports car racing with success and won Le Mans in a Peugeot in 1992 and became World Champion in this sphere the same year. He was induced back to Formula One in 1993 with the Footwork team but yet another season of struggle saw him to decide to call it a day as a professional driver.

31 GRAND PRIX FOR RENAULT

1984
Brazil: Did not finish
South Africa: 3rd
Belgium: 2nd
San Marino: 4th
France: Accident
Monaco: Accident
Canada: Did not finish
United States East:
Did not finish
United States West:
Did not finish
Great Britain: 2nd

Germany: 3rd
Austria: Did not finish
Holland: Accident
Italy: Did not finish
Europe: 11th
Portugal: Did not finish

1985
Brazil: 10th
Portugal: 7th
San Marino; 10th
Monaco: 5th
Canada: Accident

United States East:
Did not finish
France: 7th
Great Britain: 5th
Germany: Did not finish
Austria: Did not finish
Holland: Did not finish
Italy: Did not finish
Belgium: 6th
Europe: Did not finish
Australia: Did not finish

PHILIPPE STREIFF

Born 26 June 1955, La Tronche, France

Philippe first came to prominence in 1977 when he won the Volant Motul competition and so moved into Formula Renault for 1978. His initial success was winning the relevant support event at the French Grand Prix and he enjoyed a consistent year overall. This provided the platform to compete in the European Formula Three series from 1979, first in a Martini-Renault and then with Toyota for the 1980 season. He decided to concentrate on his national series in 1981 and duly won the title in an Alfa Romeo. That accomplished, Formula Two was next in his sights and from 1982 to 1984 he was always a leading contender driving for AGS. In that final year at this level he was given an outing by Renault Formula One in the Portuguese Grand Prix. He worked with Renault-powered teams for the following seasons, first with Ligier and in 1986 with Tyrell exclusively. A former team, AGS, snaffled him up but, very sadly, in 1989 while testing for them in Brazil he crashed and suffered injuries that left him paralysed.

22 GRAND PRIX FOR RENAULT, LIGIER-RENAULT AND TYRRELL-RENAULT

1984 Renault
Portugal: Did not finish

1985 Ligier-Renault
Italy: 10th
Belgium: 9th
Europe: 8th
Australia: 3rd

1985 (Tyrrell-Renault)
South Africa: Accident

1986 (Tyrrell-Renault)
Brazil: 7th
Spain: Did not finish
San Marino: Did not finish
Monaco: 11th
Belgium: 12th
Canada: 11th

United States East: 9th
France: Did not finish
Great Britain: 6th
Germany: Did not finish
Hungary: 8th
Austria: Did not finish
Italy: 9th
Portugal: Did not finish
Mexico: Did not finish
Australia: 5th

Philippe Streiff, 1986

ELIO DE ANGELIS

Born 26 March 1958, Rome, Italy
Died 15 May 1986, Paul Ricard Circuit, France

Elio made his Formula One debut at the age of twenty. This was the 1979 Argentinian Grand Prix, at the wheel of a Shadow. He was signed by Lotus the following season and came within an ace of being the youngest winner in the sport with a close second in the Brazilian Grand Prix that year. During his career at Lotus he succeeded in winning the 1982 Austrian Grand Prix and the 1985 San Marino Grand Prix. Like others he did not enjoy the best working relationship with team partner Ayrton Senna and Elio moved to Brabham for the 1986 season. He was killed during a practice session for the team at Paul Ricard.

47 GRAND PRIX FOR LOTUS-RENAULT

1983:	1984	1985
Brazil: Disqualified	Brazil: 3rd	Brazil: 3rd
United States West: Did not finish	South Africa: 7th	Portugal: 4th
France: Did not finish	Belgium: 5th	San Marino: 1st
San Marino: Did not finish	San Marino: 3rd	Monaco: 3rd
Monaco: Did not finish	France: 5th	Canada: 5th
Belgium: 9th	Monaco: 6th	United States East: 5th
United States East: Did not finish	Canada: 4th	France: 5th
Canada: Did not finish	United States East: 3rd	Great Britain: Not classified
Great Britain: Did not finish	United States West: 3rd	Germany: Did not finish
Germany: Did not finish	Great Britain: 4th	Austria: 5th
Austria: Accident	Germany: Did not finish	Holland: 5th
Holland: Did not finish	Austria: Did not finish	Italy: 6th
Italy: 5th	Holland: 4th	Belgium: Did not finish
Europe: Did not finish	Italy: Did not finish	Europe: 5th
South Africa: Did not finish	Europe: Did not finish	South Africa: Did not finish
	Portugal: 5th	Australia: Disqualified

**Elio de Angelis,
Brazilian GP,
13 March 1983**

NIGEL MANSELL

Born 8 August 1953, Upton-on-Severn, Worcestershire, England

Success came to Nigel late in his career. He had worked his way up manfully from karting through Formula Ford and into Formula Three, with budget always a challenge. Eventually he was spotted by Lotus team manager Peter Collins and given a role as a test driver. He gradually gained regular drives in Formula One with the team by 1981. Lotus became Renault-powered in 1983 but it was with Williams-Honda that he gained his first victory, at the seventy-second attempt, in 1985. He never looked back and was propelled from journeyman to one of Britain's greatest Formula One drivers. At the peak of his career as World Champion in 1992 he somehow managed to fall out with his team owner, Frank Williams, over money and status. Nigel lost his seat for the 1993 season but did manage the incredible feat of moving across the Atlantic to win the Indycar Championship in his 'rookie' year. He did return to Williams-Renault for a third chapter, briefly, with some outings in 1994, and in true style concluded his Formula One career with a victory in Australia for the final race of the season.

59 GRAND PRIX WITH LOTUS-RENAULT AND WILLIAMS-RENAULT

1983 (Lotus-Renault)
Great Britain: 4th
Germany: Did not finish
Austria: 5th
Holland: Did not finish
Italy: 8th
Europe: 3rd
South Africa: Did not finish

1984
Brazil: Accident
South Africa: Did not finish
Belgium: Did not finish
San Marino: Accident
France: 3rd
Monaco: Accident
Canada: 6th
United States East: Did not finish
United States West: 6th
Great Britain: Did not finish
Germany: 4th
Austria: Did not finish
Holland: 3rd

Italy: Accident
Europe: Did not finish
Portugal: Did not finish

1991 (Williams-Renault)
United States: Did not finish
Brazil: Did not finish
San Marino: Accident
Monaco: 2nd
Canada: 6th
Mexico: 2nd
France: 1st
Great Britain: 1st
Germany: 1st
Hungary: 2nd
Belgium: Did not finish
Italy: 1st
Portugal: Disqualified
Spain: 1st
Japan: Accident
Australia: 2nd

1992
South Africa: 1st

Mexico: 1st
Brazil: 1st
Spain: 1st
San Marino: 1st
Monaco: 2nd
Canada: Did not finish
France: 1st
Great Britain: 1st
Germany: 1st
Hungary: 2nd
Belgium: 2nd
Italy: Did not finish
Portugal: 1st
Japan: Did not finish
Australia: Accident

1994
France: Did not finish
Europe: Accident
Japan: 4th
Australia: 1st

Nigel Mansell,
South African GP,
1 March 1992

FRANCOIS HESNAULT

Born 30 December 1956, Paris, France

Francois dabbled in hill climbing before trying a more ambitious form of motor sport. After a successful training session with the Winfield School at Magny Cours in 1979 he entered Formula Renault in 1980. He proved competitive and, by 1982, Hesnault was racing in French Formula Three and was a title contender that year and the next. As a Frenchman with a portfolio of sponsors, he was signed by Ligier for the 1984 Formula One season. This was a disappointing year but he was able to pick up a seat alongside Nelson Piquet at Brabham in 1985. Soon dropped, he still managed to make history with Renault when he drove in the German Grand Prix with the first on-board camera for television viewers.

16 GRAND PRIX FOR LIGIER-RENAULT AND RENAULT

1984 (Ligier-Renault)
Brazil: Did not finish
South Africa: 10th
Belgium: Did not finish
San Marino: Accident
Monaco: Did not finish
Canada: Did not finish

United States East: Accident
United States West: Accident
Great Britain: Did not finish
Germany: 8th
Austria: 8th
Holland: 7th

Italy: Accident
Europe: 10th
Portugal: Did not finish

1985 (Renault)
Germany: Did not finish

Francois Hesnault, 1984

Andrea de Cesaris, Ligier-Renault, Brazilian GP, 25 March 1984

ANDREA DE CESARIS

Born 31 May 1959, Rome, Italy

Andrea had a promising start in motor sport. He was a World Karting Champion and racing in British Formula Three by the age of eighteen. He entered Formula One at twenty-one with Alfa Romeo in 1980 and was signed by McLaren in 1981. He did not impress his new employers and was released back to Alfa Romeo for 1982. Despite remaining an erratic performer over the next two seasons, Ligier signed him in 1984 and retained De Cesaris for 1985. The Italian then hopped from team to team for the remainder of his Formula One days. He took the wheel with Minardi, Brabham, Rial, Dallaras, Jordan, Tyrrell and Sauber. Regardless of his controversial reputation, Andrea had started 208 Grand Prix by the time he finally hung up his helmet in 1994!

27 GRAND PRIX WITH LIGIER-RENAULT

1984
Brazil: Did not finish
South Africa: 5th
Belgium: Accident
San Marino: 7th
France: 10th
Monaco: Did not finish
Canada: Did not finish
United States East: Did not finish
United States West:

Accident
Great Britain: 10th
Germany: 7th
Austria: Did not finish
Holland: Did not finish
Italy: Did not finish
Europe: 7th
Portugal: 12th

1985
Brazil: Accident

Portugal: Did not finish
San Marino: Accident
Monaco: 4th
Canada: 14th
United States: 10th
France: Did not finish
Great Britain: Did not finish
Germany: Accident
Austria: Accident
Holland: Did not finish

AYRTON SENNA

Born 21 March 1960, San Paulo, Brazil
Died 1 May 1994, Imola Circuit, Italy

Ayrton Senna da Silva is acknowledged as one of the greatest drivers in the history of the sport. A world-class karter in his formative years, his move into Formula Ford 1600 saw him a race winner from the start. He was a top performer on the European Formula Three circuits and by 1983 was accepting invitations to test with McLaren, Williams and Toleman. He signed for the latter team in 1984 but soon decided to move on to Lotus for the 1985 season. Here he enjoyed the first race victories of his career. By 1988 McLaren were able to offer him an enticing package and he was paired with Alain Prost. They became bitter rivals for the world crown and Senna often gave Prost a robust time on track. When Prost moved to Ferrari the action remained as competitive, culminating in the 1990 Japanese Grand Prix when the Brazilian took the Frenchman off and guaranteed himself the title. He had only just settled into his debut season with Williams-Renault in 1994 when the three-times World Champion suffered a fatal crash at Imola on 1 May.

35 GRAND PRIX WITH LOTUS-RENAULT AND WILLIAMS-RENAULT

1985 (Lotus-Renault)
Brazil: Did not finish
Portugal: 1st
San Marino: 7th
Monaco: Did not finish
Canada: 16th
United States East: Accident
France: Accident
Great Britain: 10th
Germany: Did not finish
Austria: 2nd
Holland: 3rd
Italy: 3rd
Belgium: 1st

Europe: 2nd
South Africa: Did not finish
Australia: Did not finish

1986
Brazil: 2nd
Spain: 1st
San Marino: Did not finish
Monaco: 3rd
Belgium: 2nd
Canada: 5th
United States East: 1st
France: Accident
Great Britain: Did not finish

Germany: 2nd
Hungary: 2nd
Austria: Did not finish
Italy: Did not finish
Portugal: 4th
Mexico: 3rd
Australia: Did not finish

1994 (Williams-Renault)
Brazil: Did not finish
Pacific: Accident
San Marino: Fatal accident

Ayrton Senna,
January 1994

JACQUES LAFITTE

Born 21 November 1943, Paris, France

Jacques was Jean-Pierre Jabouille's mechanic in the latter's early days of racing and his brother-in-law. Jacques himself came through a very competitive European Formula Three series and made his Formula One debut with Williams in 1974. He spent the bulk of his career moving between that team and Ligier, with whom he enjoyed comparative success. He sustained serious leg injuries at the 1986 British Grand Prix at Brands Hatch and never returned to Formula One. He then moved into the touring cars scene before retiring to a television career as an Formula One commentator.

24 GRAND PRIX FOR LIGIER-RENAULT

1985
Brazil: 6th
Portugal: Did not finish
San Marino: Did not finish
Monaco: 6th
Canada: 8th
United States East: 12th
France: Did not finish
Great Britain: 3rd
Germany: 3rd

Austria; Did not finish
Holland: Did not finish
Italy: Did not finish
Belgium: 11th
Europe: Did not finish
Australia: 2nd

1986
Brazil: 3rd
Spain: Did not finish

San Marino: Did not finish
Monaco: 6th
Belgium: 5th
Canada: 7th
United States: 2nd
France: 6th
Great Britain: Accident

Jaques Lafitte,
December 1989

Martin Brundle, Italian
GP, 7 September 1986

MARTIN BRUNDLE

Born 1 June 1959, King's Lynn, Norfolk, England

Martin came to the attention of the motor sport fraternity through his highly competitive clashes with Ayrton Senna in the 1983 British Formula Three Championship. Both were snapped up by Formula One teams the following season and Martin raced for Tyrrell. He was among the points across his debut season. He then enjoyed a sustained career with a variety of teams including being team partner to Michael Schumacher at Benetton and Mika Hakkinen at McLaren. After retiring at the end of the 1996 season he was signed by ITV as co-commentator for their new contract and has enjoyed a successful transition to a media career while still keeping active as a sports car driver.

40 GRAND PRIX FOR TYRRELL-RENAULT AND LIGIER-RENAULT

1985 (Tyrrell-Renault)
France: Did not finish
Great Britain: 7th
Holland: 7th
Italy: 8th
Belgium: 13th
Europe: Did not finish
South Africa: 7th
Australia: Accident

1986
Brazil: 5th
Spain: Did not finish
San Marino: 8th
Monaco: Accident
Belgium: Did not finish

Canada: 9th
United States East: Did not finish
France: 10th
Great Britain: 5th
Germany: Did not finish
Hungary: 6th
Austria: Did not finish
Italy: 10th
Portugal: Did not finish
Mexico: 11th
Australia: 4th

1993 (Ligier-Renault)
South Africa: Accident
Brazil: Accident

Europe: Did not finish
San Marino: 3rd
Spain: Accident
Monaco: 6th
Canada: 5th
France: 5th
Great Britain: 14th
Germany: 8th
Hungary: 5th
Belgium: 7th
Italy: Accident
Portugal: 6th
Japan: 9th
Australia: 6th

STEFAN BELLOF

Born 20 November 1957, Giessen, Germany
Died 1 September 1985, Spa-Francorchamps Circuit, Belgium

Stefan Bellof was regarded as a great prospect when he signed for Ken Tyrrell in 1984 after an outstanding Formula Two background. He sadly lost his life in sports car racing at Spa when contesting the lead and crashing at Eau Rouge.

3 GRAND PRIX FOR TYRRELL-RENAULT

1985
Germany: 8th
Austria: 7th
Holland: Did not finish

Ivan Capelli, 1985

Stefan Bellof, 1985

IVAN CAPELLI

Born 24 May 1963, Milan, Italy

Ivan graduated from karting through the Italian Formula Three series as champion and into the European series, which he also won in 1984. He made his Formula One debut the following year with Tyrrell-Renault while also competing in the European Formula 3000 series, where he claimed a title in 1986.

Despite opportunities with a variety of teams, including Ferrari, he never matched the performances of his formative years in motor sport and by the mid-1990s had retired into media work around the Formula One scene.

2 GRAND PRIX WITH TYRELL-RENAULT

1985
Europe: Accident
Australia: 4th

Johnny Dumfries,
1986

PHILIPPE ALLIOT

Born 27 July 1954, near Chartres, France

Philippe had both elite military training and a course at university behind him when he turned his attention to motor racing. He vied with Alain Prost for top spot in Formula Renault before winning the championship in 1978 and moving into French Formula Three. He then went on into the European series in the late 1970s. He was a successful sports car driver in the early 1980s before making his Formula One debut with RAM in 1985. Replacing the injured Laffite at Ligier in 1986, he then spent several seasons with Larrousse Lola. A very successful return to sports car racing in the 1990s was followed by retirement to combine media work with political aspirations.

7 GRAND PRIX FOR LIGIER-RENAULT

1986

Germany: Did not finish	Portugal: Did not finish
Hungary: 9th	Mexico: 6th
Austria: Did not finish	Australia: 8th
Italy: Did not finish	

Philippe Alliot,
1986

JOHNNY DUMFRIES
(LORD CRICHTON, MARQUIS OF BUTE)

Born 26 April 1958, Isle of Bute, Scotland

Born into great wealth, Johnny could have settled for a less demanding lifestyle than racing motor cars! He entered motor sport by an assumed name and without budget to ensure a normal edge to his activities. He sought sponsorship to race in Formula Ford 1600 before proving capable of competing in Formula Three against the likes of Senna and Brundle. He managed to win the British Championship series in 1984 and was second in the European series to Capelli the same season. His first Formula One experience was as a test driver for Ferrari while he was also racing in Formula 3000. This led to a full-time seat with Lotus-Renault for 1986. He eventually enjoyed success in sports car racing with Jaguar, winning the Spa 1000 in 1987 and the Le Mans 24-Hours in 1988.
   Succeeding to the family titles in 1993, he now sits in the House of Lords.

15 GRAND PRIX FOR LOTUS-RENAULT

1986

Brazil: 9th	United States East: 7th	Italy: Did not finish
Spain: Did not finish	France: Did not finish	Portugal: 9th
San Marino: Did not finish	Great Britain: 7th	Mexico: Did not finish
Belgium: Accident	Germany: Did not finish	Australia: 6th
Canada: Accident	Hungary: 5th	
	Austria: Did not finish	

**Riccardo Patrese,
January 1989**

THIERRY BOUTSEN

Born 13 July 1957, Brussels, Belgium

Thierry was studying to be an engineer but his interest in racing cars took over. He came to prominence in 1978 when taking the Benelux FF1600 title. This was the springboard to the European Formula Three scene where he was signed by Martini. By 1981 he was in Formula Two with March-BMW. He enjoyed successful outings in sports car racing from 1983 while also entering Formula One with Arrows. He joined Williams-Renault in 1989 from Benetton and won the Canadian and Australian Grand Prix in his first season with them. Moving to Ligier-Renault, he finished his Formula One career at Jordan. Afterwards he raced in sports cars for several seasons but never returned after a major pile-up at the 1999 Le Mans event.

48 GRAND PRIX FOR WILLIAMS-RENAULT AND LIGIER-RENAULT

1989 (Williams-Renault))	1990	1992 (Ligier-Renault)
Brazil: Did not finish	United States: 3rd	South Africa: Did not finish
San Marino: 4th	Brazil: 5th	Mexico: 10th
Monaco: 10th	San Marino: Did not finish	Brazi: Accident
Mexico: Did not finish	Monaco: 4th	Spain: Did not finish
United States: 6th	Canada: Accident	San Marino: Did not finish
Canada: 1st	Mexico: 5th	Monaco: 12th
France: Did not finish	France: Did not finish	Canada: 10th
Great Britain: 10th	Great Britain: 2nd	France: Did not finish
Germany: Accident	Germany: 6th	Great Britain: 10th
Hungary: 3rd	Hungary: 1st	Germany: 7th
Belgium: 4th	Belgium: Did not finish	Hungary: Accident
Italy: 3rd	Italy: Did not finish	Belgium: Accident
Portugal: Did not finish	Portugal: Did not finish	Italy: Did not finish
Spain: Did not finish	Spain: 4th	Portugal: 8th
Japan: 3rd	Japan: 5th	Japan: Did not finish
Australia: 1st	Australia: 5th	Australia: 5th

**Thierry Boutsen,
January 1989**

RICCARDO PATRESE

Born 17 April 1954, Padua, Italy

Riccardo enjoyed longevity in the sport and by the time he retired he had competed in 256 Grand Prix between 1977 and 1993, what is also remarkable also is the span of his race victories from his maiden one in 1982 at Monaco to his final triumph at the Japanese GP in 1992. He drove for several teams in his long career but was most successful with Williams-Renault from 1989 to 1992.

64 GRAND PRIX FOR WILLIAMS-RENAULT

1989		
Brazil: Did not finish	Mexico: 9th	Italy: Did not finish
San Marino: Did not finish	France: 6th	Portugal: 1st
Monaco: 15th	Great Britain: Did not finish	Spain: 3rd
Mexico: 2nd	Germany: 5th	Japan: 3rd
United States: 2nd	Hungary: 4th	Australia: 5th
Canada: 2nd	Belgium: Did not finish	
France: 3rd	Italy: 5th	**1992**
Great Britain: Did not finish	Portugal: 7th	South Africa: 2nd
Germany: Did not finish	Spain: 5th	Mexico: 2nd
Hungary: Did not finish	Japan: 4th	Brazil: 2nd
Belgium: Accident	Australia: 6th	Spain: Accident
Italy: 4th		San Marino: 2nd
Portugal: did not finish	**1991**	Monaco: 3rd
Spain: 5th	United States: Accident	Canada: Did not finish
Japan: 2nd	Brazil: 2nd	France: 2nd
Australia: 3rd	San Marino: Did not finish	Great Britain: 2nd
	Monaco: Accident	Germany: 8th
1990	Canada: 3rd	Hungary: Did not finish
United States: 9th	Mexico: 1st	Belgium: 3rd
Brazil: 13th	France: 5th	Italy: 5th
San Marino: 1st	Great Britain: Accident	Portugal: Accident
Monaco: Did not finish	Germany: 2nd	Japan: 1st
Canada: Did not finish	Hungary: 3rd	Australia: Did not finish
	Belgium: 5th	

Erik Comas, January 1994

MARK BLUNDELL

Born 8 April 1966, Barnet, Hertfordshire, England

Mark made an immediate impact in his debut season in 1984. He finished second in the Junior FF1600 series and won the Champion of Snetterton title. The following year Mark won the BBC Grandstand FF2000 championship. By the end of 1986 he was European Formula Ford Champion. However, he spent a couple of unfulfilled seasons in Formula 3000 before changing to sports car racing in 1990 and also gaining a test drive with Williams. He made his Formula One start for Brabham in 1991 and had seasons with Ligier-Renault in 1993 and McLaren in 1994. He then crossed to the CART scene in America and survived a major crash to race on to the end of the 2000 season.

16 GRAND PRIX FOR LIGIER-RENAULT

1993		
South Africa: 3rd	Monaco: Accident	Belgium: 11th
Brazil: 5th	Canada: Accident	Italy: Accident
Europe: Accident	France: Accident	Portugal: Accident
San Marino: Accident	Great Britain: 7th	Japan: 7th
Spain: 7th	Germany: 3rd	Australia: 9th
	Hungary: 7th	

Mark Blundell, February 1993

ERIK COMAS

Born 28 September 1963, near Valence, France

Erik came through the ranks competing in kart racing, Formula Renault, French Formula Three and Formula 3000. He joined Ligier in 1991 and moved to Larrouse in 1993, and competed in Japanese sports car racing from 1994.

15 GRAND PRIX FOR LIGIER-RENAULT

1992		
South Africa: 7th	Monaco: 10th	Italy: Accident
Mexico: 9th	Canada: 6th	Portugal: Did not finish
Brazil: Did not finish	France: 5th	Japan: Did not finish
Spain: Accident	Great Britain: 8th	Australia: Did not finish
San Marino: 9th	Germany: 6th	
	Hungary: Accident	

DAMON HILL

Born 17 September 1960, London, England

Despite being the son of Formula One World Champion Graham Hill, Damon did not have an early and smooth passage into the sport. He preferred to race bikes in his younger days, and money was not plentiful. He only entered four-wheel racing in his mid-twenties with a tentative start in Formula Ford. He moved through Formula Three and eventually into Formula 3000, making gradual progress. Damon became increasingly competitive and was given a chance by Frank Williams as a test driver for the team. He proved most diligent and, importantly, also showed he had genuine pace. Drives were arranged with Brabham for the 1992 season with that team in steep decline, and so it was a real challenge for Damon to even qualify. When Nigel Mansell could not agree terms to return for the 1993 season with Williams it was decided to give Hill his chance. Although second string to the great Alain Prost, the Englishman soon proved to be a front-runner too. After a series of unlucky near misses Damon registered his first victory that season in Hungary and, with more to follow, finished third in the World Championship. When Prost retired, Hill was now paired with another legend. Ayrton Senna, however, was killed in a track crash at Imola on 1 May. In the most difficult of circumstances Damon Hill was thrust into the role of team leader. He rose to the challenge manfully and only ,issed out on the title by 1 point to Michael Schumacher. That was in the most controversial of circumstances when the German pushed him off the circuit in the final race at Adelaide. He remained the main competitor to Schmacher in 1995 and the presence of a bright new teammate, Jacques Villeneuve, took his efforts to an even greater dimension in 1996 when he emulated his father to become World Champion.

65 GRAND PRIX FOR WILLIAMS-RENAULT

1993
South Africa: Accident
Brazil: 2nd
Europe: 2nd
San Marino: Accident
Spain: Accident
Monaco: 2nd
Canada: 3rd
France: 2nd
Great Britain: Did not finish
Germany: 15th
Hungary: 1st
Belgium: 1st
Italy: 1st
Portugal: 3rd
Japan: 4th
Australia: 3rd

1994
Brazil: 2nd
Pacific: Did not finish
San Marino: 6th
Monaco: Accident
Spain: 1st

Canada: 2nd
France: 2nd
Great Britain: 1st
Germany: 8th
Hungary: 2nd
Belgium: 1st
Italy: 1st
Portugal: 1st
Europe: 2nd
Japan: 1st
Australia: Accident

1995
Brazil: Did not finish
Argentina: 1st
San Marino: 1st
Spain: 4th
Monaco: 2nd
Canada: Did not finish
France: 2nd
Great Britain: Accident
Germany: Accident
Hungary: 1st
Belgium: 2nd

Italy: Accident
Portugal: 3rd
Europe: Accident
Pacific: 3rd
Japan: Accident
Australia: 1st

1996:
Australia: 1st
Brazil: 1st
Argentina: 1st
Europe: 4th
San Marino: 1st
Monaco: Did not finish
Spain: Accident
Canada: 1st
France: 1st
Great Britain: Accident
Germany: 1st
Hungary: 2nd
Belgium: 5th
Italy: Accident
Portugal: 2nd
Japan: 1st

Damon Hill,
South African GP,
14 March 1993

That was the real peak of his career, as his contract was not renewed and he moved to lowly Arrows. He showed his class in the Hungarian Grand Prix by leading the field into the final lap when mechanical gremlins slowed him sufficiently for Jacques Villeneuve to deny him a remarkable victory. He did, however, bring Jordan home for their first and his twenty-second win at Spa in 1998.

ERIC BARNARD

Born 26 August 1964, Istres, France

Eric started racing in karts and was a multi-champion in his home country. In 1983 he won the Volant Elf drivers' competition and the prize was a sponsored seat in Formula Renault for the following season. Within two years he was the title holder. This led to French Formula Three and he was a front-runner for two years. Formula 3000 from 1988 was equally successful and so Larousse gave him outings in Formula One in 1989 before signing him permanently. He suffered serious leg injuries in 1991 which kept him out until 1994 when Ligier-Renault reintroduced Barnard for a season. After that the Frenchman moved to a competitive career in sports car racing.

13 GRAND PRIX FOR LIGIER-RENAULT

1994
Brazil: Accident	Spain: 8th	Hungary: 10th
Pacific: 10th	Canada: 13th	Belgium: 10th
San Marino: 12th	France: Did not finish	Italy: 7th
Monaco: Did not finish	Great Britain: 13th	Portugal: 10th
	Germany: 3rd	

Eric Barnard, 1994

Olivier Panis, German GP, 31 July 1994

OLIVIER PANIS

Born 21 September 1966, Lyon, France

Olivier first raced in karts before moving through the junior formulae and then into French Formula Three. He was always a competitive front runner and Formula 3000 eventually beckoned.

His title victory in 1993 meant Ligier-Renault moved to bring him into the 1994 Formula One season. He was a consistent performer and the highlight of his debut season was second place at the German Grand Prix. In 1996 Olivier gave fans a race to remember when he took his Ligier from 14th on the grid at Monaco to victory. That was his peak – serious injury when driving for Prost at Canada in 1997 saw his opportunities come back slowly before Toyota looked to him for experienced leadership.

16 GRAND PRIX FOR LIGIER-RENAULT

1994
Brazil: 11th	Canada: 12th	Italy: 10th
Pacific: 9th	France: Accident	Portugal: Disqualified
San Marino: 11th	Great Britain: 12th	Europe: 9th
Monaco: 9th	Germany: 2nd	Japan: 11th
Spain: 7th	Hungary: 6th	Australia: 5th
	Belgium: 7th	

DAVID COULTHARD

Born 27 March 1971, Twynholm, Scotland

David was a very successful in kart racing as a youngster. He entered Formula Ford at seventeen and again proved masterful. Paul Stewart Racing moved in to sign David to race in various formulae and by the time he was nineteen he was testing for McLaren. The 1991 Formula Three series saw a season-long battle with Rubens Barrichello, Coulthard only just being pipped to the title. He entered Formula 3000 racing in 1992 and a second-year switch from PSR to Pacific Racing ensured a string of victories. This brought him to the attention of Williams-Renault and David became test driver for their 1994 season. The tragic death of Ayrton Senna meant sudden elevation for the young Scotsman. He proved competitive from the start but was frustrated by Williams deciding to alternate him with their former champion Nigel Mansell, so he took up an option with McLaren from 1996 and enjoyed a sustained career with them as a World Championship contender.

25 GRAND PRIX FOR WILLIAMS-RENAULT

1994	1995	
Spain: Did not finish	Brazil: 2nd	Germany: 2nd
Canada: 5th	Argentina: Did not finish	Hungary: 2nd
Great Britain: 5th	San Marino: 4th	Belgium: Did not finish
Germany: Did not finish	Spain: Did not finish	Italy: Accident
Hungary: Accident	Monaco: Did not finish	Portugal: 1st
Belgium: 4th	Canada: Did not finish	Europe: 3rd
Italy: 6th	France: 3rd	Pacific: 2nd
Portugal: 2nd	Great Britain: 3rd	Japan: Accident
		Australia: Accident

Frank Lagorce,
1994

David Coulthard,
British GP,
10 July 1994

FRANK LAGORCE

Born 1 September 1968, near Paris, France

Frank was a champion karter as an early teenager. He eventually went into Formula Ford 1600 at the age of twenty. His next step was in Formula Renault from 1990 and then he was French Formula Three champion in 1992. By the time of his Formula One debut with Ligier-Renault in 1994 he was enjoying a successful time in Formula 3000.

2 GRAND PRIX FOR LIGIER-RENAULT

1994
Japan: Accident
Australia: 11th

JOHNNY HERBERT

Born 25 June 1964, Brentwood, Essex, England

Johnny moved with victorious ease through karting, Formula Ford, Formula Three and Formula 3000. When given test drives with Benetton-Ford and Lotus, he was faster than the accomplished team members. The path to glory seemed very smooth. He had been lined up to sign for Williams-Renault for the 1989 season when he was the victim of an appalling pile-up at Brands Hatch in August 1988. His feet were severely broken in the incident and were to trouble him from that day onwards. He grimly fought through pain and a certain amount of immobility to amaze the Formula One paddock by finishing fourth for Benetton on his debut at the 1989 Brazilian Grand Prix. Their new team manager was Peter Collins, who had just moved from Williams and who had kept faith with Johnny. However, Collins was eventually overruled by Flavio Briatore and Johnny was moved out. He was rescued again by Collins when his mentor moved to Lotus. The team ran into financial difficulties after a couple of seasons and so Johnny did the rounds briefly with Ligier-Renault and then ironically with Benetton-Renault, where he enjoyed success despite the domination of team partner Michael Schumacher. He moved on to Stewart and enjoyed victory there before diversifying since 2001 into a variety of motor sports.

18 GRAND PRIX WITH LIGIER-RENAULT AND BENETTON-RENAULT

1994 (Ligier-Renault)
Europe: 8th

1995 (Benetton-Renault)
Brazil: Accident
Argentina: 4th
San Marino: 7th

Spain: 2nd
Monaco: 4th
Canada: Accident
France: Accident
Great Britain: 1st
Germany: 4th
Hungary: 4th

Belgium: 7th
Italy: 1st
Portugal: 7th
Europe: 5th
Pacific: 6th
Japan: 3rd
Australia: Did not finish

Johnny Herbert,
Brazilian GP,
26 March 1995

Michael Schumacher,
February 1995

MICHAEL SCHUMACHER

Born 3 January 1969, Kerpen, Germany

Michael graduated from the karting scene to eventually win the German Formula Three Championship in 1990. At the time he was a competitive contemporary of Heinz-Harald Frentzen and Karl Wendlinger. All three were signed together to drive Sauber-Mercedes Group C sports cars. Michael was spotted by Eddie Jordan and given his Formula One debut at Spa in 1991. He qualified seventh and was snaffled from under Jordan's nose by Benetton. He began winning races for his new employers in the 1992 season and the rest, as they say, is history. His first World Championship in 1994 was shrouded in controversy both on and off the track – especially his clashes with Damon Hill. However, he had the same Renault engine as Hill in 1995 and his second title was better received. Ferrari lured him from Benetton to revive their fortunes. By 2000, after some close chases, Schumacher gave the Italian team their first World Champion since Jody Scheckter in 1979. By 2004 the German had taken his tally of individual World titles to a record-breaking total of seven.

17 GRAND PRIX FOR BENETTON-RENAULT

1995
Brazil: 1st
Argentina: 3rd
San Marino: Accident
Spain: 1st
Monaco: 1st

Canada: 5th
France: 1st
Great Britain: Accident
Germany: 1st
Hungary: 11th
Belgium: 1st

Italy: Accident
Portugal: 2nd
Europe: 1st
Pacific: 1st
Japan: 1st
Australia: Accident

JEAN ALESI

Born 11 June 1964, Avignon, France

Jean had a very successful start to his motor racing in both Formula Three, where he became French champion and Formula 3000. He entered Formula One in 1989, initially with Jordan before switching to Tyrrell. Proving an exciting racer on the circuit, he was signed by Ferrari, with whom he spent five years. He then brought this experience to Benetton-Renault in 1996 and 1997. The end of his career saw him in a rather frustrating situation with middle-order teams such as Sauber, Prost and Jordan. He is still active as a driver in the German Touring Car Championship with Mercedes-Benz.

33 GRAND PRIX WITH BENETTON-RENAULT

1996
Australia: Accident
Brazil: 2nd
Argentina: 3rd
Europe: Accident
San Marino: 6th
Monaco: Did not finish
Spain: 2nd
Canada: 3rd
France: 3rd
Great Britain: Did not finish
Germany: 2nd

Hungary: 3rd
Belgium: 4th
Italy: 2nd
Portugal: 4th
Japan: Accident

1997
Australia: Did not finish
Brazil: 6th
Argentina: 7th
San Marino: 5th
Monaco: Did not finish

Spain: 3rd
Canada: 2nd
France: 5th
Great Britain: 2nd
Germany: 6th
Hungary: 11th
Belgium: 8th
Italy: 2nd
Austria: Accident
Luxembourg: 2nd
Japan: 5th
Europe: 15th

Jean Alesi,
European GP,
28 April 1996

Gerhard Berger,
Argentinian GP,
7 April 1996

GERHARD BERGER

Born 27 August 1959, Worgl, Austria

Gerhard moved quickly through Formula Ford and into the German and European Formula Three competitions. His talent was quickly spotted and ATS gave him his Formula One debut in 1984. Arrows snapped him up for 1985 with Benetton offering him a place for 1986. He was upwardly mobile again. He gained his maiden victory with the latter team at Mexico in 1986 and it was inevitable the very top teams would want his services. He served both Ferrari and McLaren as a race winner before returning to Benetton-Renault in 1996 to see out his career in style and provide that team with his foresight and feedback. He retired into management with Williams-BMW, being in charge of their competition programme.

30 GRAND PRIX FOR BENETTON-RENAULT

1996
Australia: 4th
Brazil: Did not finish
Argentina: Did not finish
Europe: 9th
San Marino: 3rd
Monaco: Did not finish
Spain: Did not finish
Canada: Did not finish
France: 4th
Great Britain: 2nd

Germany: 13th
Hungary: Did not finish
Belgium: 6th
Italy: Did not finish
Portugal: 6th
Japan: 4th

1997
Australia: 4th
Brazil: 2nd
Argentina: 6th

San Marino: Accident
Monaco: 9th
Spain: 10th
Germany: 1st
Hungary: 8th
Belgium: 6th
Italy: 7th
Austria: 10th
Luxembourg: 4th
Japan: 8th
Europe: 4th

JACQUES VILLENEUVE

Born 9 April 1971, St Jean sur Richelieu, Canada

Jacques' father Gilles was a Grand Prix driver of great repute who was killed on-track in 1982. Despite this tragedy, the young Jacques was determined to follow in Gilles' tread marks. He graduated from Formula Three in Japan to contest the American Formula Atlantic Championship. This he won and moved to Indy Car Racing in 1994. Jacques was an outstanding success. By 1995 he had won the Indycar Championship and the famous Indy 500. Williams-Renault was able to offer him a top seat for 1996 in Formula One. The young Canadian's impact was immediate. He put his car on pole position in the first race of the season at Melbourne and was leading until five laps from the flag before an oil leak meant his caution saw teammate Damon Hill through for victory. Jacques did register four race victories that season, however, before his performances in 1997 took him to World Champion in only his second season in the sport. He joined his manager Craig Pollock in forming BAR in 1999 and remained, despite management changes, until the end of the 2003 season – but at the wrong end of the grid for a racer of his ability. He re-entered F1 with Sauber in 2005.

33 GRAND PRIX FOR WILLIAMS-RENAULT

1996
Australia: 2nd
Brazil: Accident
Argentina: 2nd
Europe: 1st
San Marino: 11th
Monaco: Accident
Spain: 3rd
Canada: 2nd
France: 2nd
Great Britain: 1st
Germany: 3rd

Hungary: 1st
Belgium: 2nd
Italy: 7th
Portugal: 1st
Japan: Accident

1997
Australia: Accident
Brazil: 1st
Argentina: 1st
San Marino: Did not finish
Monaco: Accident

Spain: 1st
Canada: Accident
France: 4th
Great Britain: 1st
Germany: Did not finish
Hungary: 1st
Belgium: 5th
Italy: 5th
Austria: 1st
Luxembourg: 1st
Japan: Disqualified
Europe: 3rd

Jacques Villeneuve, Australian GP, 10 March 1996

Heinz-Harald Frentzen, 1997

HEINZ-HARALD FRENTZEN

Born 18 May 1967, Moenchengladbach, Germany

Heinz-Harald was a contemporary of Michael Schumacher in their formative years on the German motor racing scene, with the added proviso that, at that stage, he was generally the superior performer. They were rivals in the German Formula Three competition of the late 1980s and then team partners with Mercedes-Benz in World sports cars. Frentzen also had a greater versatility in a number of other formulae in which he successfully participated. However, he decided to leave sports cars and his team and take part in Formula 3000 in Japan. By the time Heinz-Harald had returned, his compatriot had made his sensational debut for Jordan in the 1991 Belgian GP and been snapped up by Benetton for the 1992 Formula One campaign. It was 1994 before Heinz-Harald had his chance to enter Formula One with Sauber. He performed well for the fledgling team and at the end of the 1996 season Frank Williams controversially drafted him in to replace new World Champion Damon Hill. This was the big opportunity but he did not gel with his British engineers and moved to Jordan at the end of his contract in 1998, ironically to team up with Hill! He became team leader in 2000 and finished third in the World Championship. His time at Jordan suddenly finished in acrimony midway through 2001. He joined Arrows for 2002, who went out of business owing him money. 2003 saw Heinz-Harald complete the loop of his career back at Sauber.

17 GRAND PRIX WITH WILLIAMS-RENAULT

1997
Australia: 8th
Brazil: 9th
Argentina: Did not finish
San Marino: 1st
Monaco: Accident

Spain: 8th
Canada: 4th
France: 2nd
Great Britain: Accident
Germany: Accident
Hungary: Did not finish

Belgium: 3rd
Italy: 3rd
Austria: 3rd
Luxembourg: 3rd
Japan: 2nd
Europe: 6th

ALEXANDER WURZ

Born 15 February 1974, Waidhofen, Austria

Alexander has the distinction of being a world champion – as a BMX cyclist! He was very much a journeyman in his formative years in motor sport but looked good in German Formula Three in 1994. He came to real prominence in 1996 as the youngest winner of the Le Mans 24-Hours race, driving a Porsche. This, plus good sponsorship support, attracted the attention of Benetton-Renault, who needed cover for Gerhard Berger during part of the 1997 season. This landed him a full-time contract with the team, with whom he remained until 2000. In recent seasons he has been a test driver for McLaren.

3 GRAND PRIX FOR BENETTON-RENAULT

1997
Canada: Did not finish
France: Did not finish
Great Britain: 3rd

Alexander Wurz,
1997

Vital Statistics

OF 286 GRAND PRIX TO 1997

SIX WORLD CONSTRUCTORS' TITLES

1992 Team Williams-Renault

1993 Team Williams-Renault

1994 Team Williams-Renault

1995 Team Benetton-Renault

1996 Team Williams-Renault

1997 Team Williams-Renault

FIVE WORLD DRIVERS' TITLES

1992 Nigel Mansell with Williams-Renault

1993 Alain Prost with Williams-Renault

1995 Michael Schumacher with
Benetton-Renault

1996 Damon Hill with Williams-Renault

1997 Jacques Villeneuve with Williams-Renault

Formula Renault World Champions. Louis Schweitzer, 3 November 1997

Hungarian GP, 15 August 1993

Damon Hill, British GP,
10 July 1994

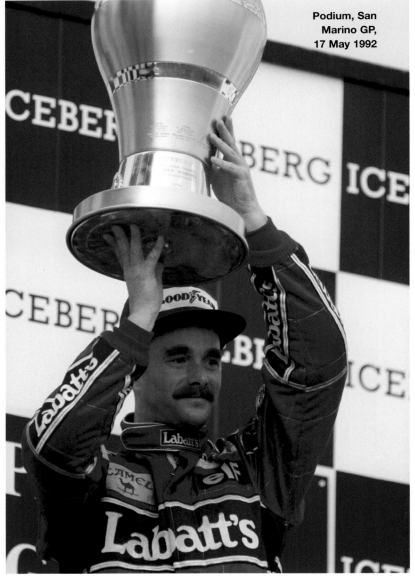

Podium, San
Marino GP,
17 May 1992

WINS PER DRIVER

DAMON HILL: 21
1993 Hungary, Belgium, Italy
1994 Spain, Great Britain, Belgium, Italy, Portugal, Japan
1995 Argentina, San Marino, Hungary, Australia
1996 Australia, Brazil, Argentina, San Marino, Canada, France, Germany, Japan

ALAIN PROST: 16
1981 France, Holland, Italy
1982 South Africa, Brazil
1983 France, Belgium, Great Britain, Austria
1993 South Africa, San Marino, Spain, Canada, France, Great Britain, Germany

NIGEL MANSELL: 15
1991 France, Great Britain, Germany, Italy, Spain
1992 South Africa, Mexico, Brazil, Spain, San Marino, France, Great Britain, Germany, Portugal
1993 Australia

JACQUES VILLENEUVE: 11
1996 Europe, Great Britain, Hungary, Portugal
1997 Brazil, Argentina, Spain, Great Britain, Hungary, Austria, Luxembourg

MICHAEL SCHUMACHER: 9
1995 Brazil, Spain, Monaco, France, Germany, Belgium, Europe, Pacific, Japan

Australian GP,
7 November 1993

AYRTON SENNA: 4
1985 Portugal, Belgium
1986 Spain, United States East

RENE ARNOUX: 4
1980 Brazil, South Africa
1982 France, Italy

RICCARDO PATRESE: 4
1990 San Marino
1991 Mexico, Portugal
1992 Japan

THIERRY BOUTSEN: 3
1989 Canada, Australia
1990 Hungary

JEAN-PIERRE JABOUILLE: 2
1979 France
1980 Austria

JOHNNY HERBERT: 2
1995 Great Britain, Italy

ELIO DE ANGELIS: 1
1985 San Marino

DAVID COULTHARD: 1
1995 Portugal

HEINZ-HARALD FRENTZEN: 1
1997 San Marino

GERHARD BERGER: 1
1997 Germany

Lotus-Renault,
Belgian GP,
25 March 1986

**Austrian GP,
12 August 1979**

POLE POSITIONS PER DRIVER

ALAIN PROST: 23
1981 Germany, Holland
1982 Brazil, Belgium, United States East, Switzerland, United States West
1983 France, Monaco, Belgium
1993 South Africa, Brazil, Europe, San Marino, Spain, Monaco, Canada, Great Britain, Germany, Hungary, Belgium, Italy, Japan

DAMON HILL: 20
1993 France, Portugal
1994 France, Great Britain
1995 Brazil, Monaco, Great Britain, Germany, Hungary, Australia
1996 Brazil, Argentina, Europe, Spain, Canada, Great Britain, Germany, Italy, Portugal

NIGEL MANSELL: 18
1984 United Staates East
1991 Great Britain, Germany
1992 South Africa, Mexico, Brazil, Spain, San Marino, Monaco, France, Great Britain, Germany, Belgium, Italy, Portugal, Japan, Australia
1994 Pacific

AYRTON SENNA: 18
1985 Portugal, San Marino, Monaco, United States East, Italy, Europe, Australia
1986 Brazil, Spain, San Marino, United States East, France, Hungary, Portugal, Mexico

RENE ARNOUX: 14
1979 Austria, Holland
1980 Austria, Holland, Italy
1981 France, Great Britain, Austria, Italy
1982 South Africa, San Marino, Monaco, Holland, France

JACQUES VILLENEUVE: 13
1996 Australia, Belgium, Japan
1997 Australia, Brazil, Argentina, San Marino,

Nigel Mansell,
Lotus-Renault, French GP,
20 May 1984

Spain, Great Britain, Belgium, Austria, Japan, Europe

JEAN-PIERRE JABOUILLE: 6
1979 South Africa, France, Germany, Italy
1980 Brazil, South Africa

RICCARDO PATRESE: 6
1989 Hungary
1991 Canada, Mexico, France, Portugal
1992 Hungary

DAVID COULTHARD: 5
1995 Argentina, Italy, Portugal, Europe, Pacific

MICHAEL SCHUMACHER: 4
1995 San Marino, Spain, Canada (Renault's 100th pole position), Japan

ELIO DE ANGELIS: 3
1983 Europe
1984 Brazil
1985 Canada

PATRICK TAMBAY: 1
1984 France

THIERRY BOUTSEN: 1
1990 Hungary

HEINZ-HARALD FRENTZEN: 1
1997 Monaco

GERHARD BERGER: 1
1997 Germany

JEAN ALESI: 1
1997 Italy

**Italian GP,
14 September 1980**

FASTEST LAPS PER DRIVER

DAMON HILL: 18
1993 Great Britain, Italy, Portugal, Australia
1994 France, Great Britain, Belgium, Italy, Japan
1995 Spain, Great Britain, Hungary, Australia
1996 Brazil, Europe, San Marino, Germany, Hungary

NIGEL MANSELL: 15
1983 Europe
1991 Brazil, Canada, Mexico, France, Great Britain, Portugal

1992 South Africa, Spain, Monaco, France, Great Britain, Hungary, Italy, Japan

ALAIN PROST: 14
1981 France
1982 South Africa, Great Britain, Austria
1983 France, Great Britain, Austria
1993 South Africa, San Marino, Monaco, Hungary, Belgium, Japan

RICCARDO PATRESE: 10
1989 Brazil

1990 Hungary, Portugal, Spain, Japan
1991 Germany, Spain
1992 Brazil, San Marino, Germany

JACQUES VILLENEUVE: 9
1996 Australia, Canada, France, Great Britain, Portugal, Japan
1997 Brazil, Belgium, Germany

RENE ARNOUX: 8
1979 France, Austria
1980 Brazil, South Africa, Austria, Holland
1981 Great Britain
1982 Italy

MICHAEL SCHUMACHER: 8
1995 Brazil, Argentina, Canada, France, Germany, Europe, Pacific, Japan

HEINZ-HARALD FRENTZEN: 6
1997 Australia, San Marino, Hungary, Luxembourg, Japan, Europe

DAVID COULTHARD: 4
1994 Germany, Portugal
1995 Belgium, Portugal

AYRTON SENNA: 3
1985 Portugal, Canada, United States East

GERHARD BERGER: 3
1996 Belgium
1997 Argentina, Germany

JEAN ALESI: 2
1996 Argentina, Monaco

PATRICK TAMBAY: 1
1984 South Africa

DEREK WARWICK: 1
1984 United States East

JACQUES LAFITTE: 1
1985 Europe

THIERRY BOUTSEN: 1
1990 Germany

POINTS SCORED PER DRIVER

Damon Hill:	326
Alain Prost:	233
Nigel Mansell:	215
Riccardo Patrese:	172
Jacques Villeneuve:	159
Michael Schumacher:	102
Rene Arnoux:	99
Ayrton Senna:	93
Jean Alesi:	83
Thierry Boutsen:	73
Elio De Angelis:	69
David Coulthard:	63
Gerhard Berger:	48
Johnny Herbert:	45
Heinz-Harald Frentzen:	42
Jacques Lafitte:	30
Derek Warwick:	28
Partick Tambay:	22
Eddie Cheever:	22
Jean-Pierre Jabouille:	21
Martin Brundle:	21
Olivier Panis:	9
Phillippe Streiff:	7
Erik Comas:	4
Eric Bernard:	4
Alexander Wurz:	4
Johnny Dumfries:	3
Ivan Capelli:	3
Philippe Alliot:	1

Austrian GP, 12 August 1979

RENAULT VICTORIES PER NATIONAL GP

France: 9
Great Britain: 8
Spain, San Marino: 7
Italy, Portugal, Brazil, Germany: 6
Belgium, Hungary: 5
Australia, South Africa, Japan: 4
Canada, Argentina, Austria: 3
Mexico, Europe: 2
USA, Holland, Monaco, Pacific, Luxembourg: 1

TRIPLE CROWNS WITH RENAULT POWER

(Triple Crown: pole position, victory and fastest lap in the course of the same Grand Prix)

FRANCE 1979 RENAULT
Victory and pole position for Jabouille. Fastest lap for Arnoux.

BRAZIL 1980 RENAULT
Victory and fastest lap for Arnoux. Pole position for Jabouille.

SOUTH AFRICA 1980 RENAULT
Victory and fastest lap for Arnoux. Pole position for Jabouille.

AUSTRIA 1980 RENAULT
Victory for Jabouille. Pole position and fastest lap for Arnoux.

FRANCE 1981 RENAULT
Victory and fastest lap for Prost. Pole position for Arnoux.

SOUTH AFRICA 1982 RENAULT
Victory and fastest lap for Prost. Pole position for Arnoux.

BRAZIL 1982 RENAULT
Pole position, victory and fastest lap for Prost.

FRANCE 1983 RENAULT
Pole position, victory and fastest lap for Prost.

PORTUGAL 1985 LOTUS-RENAULT
Pole position, victory and fastest lap for Senna.

HUNGARY 1990 WILLIAMS-RENAULT
Victory and pole position for Boutsen. Fastest lap for Patrese.

Austrian GP,
12 August 1979

MEXICO 1991 WILLIAMS-RENAULT
Victory and pole position for Patrese. Fastest lap for Mansell.

FRANCE 1991 WILLIAMS-RENAULT
Victory and fastest lap for Mansell. Pole position for Patrese.

GREAT BRITAIN 1991 WILLIAMS-RENAULT
Pole position, victory and fastest lap for Mansell.

GERMANY 1991 WILLIAMS-RENAULT
Victory and pole position for Mansell. Fastest lap for Patrese.

PORTUGAL 1991
Victory and pole position for Patrese. Fastest lap for Mansell.

SOUTH AFRICA 1992 WILLIAMS-RENAULT
Pole position, victory and fastest lap for Mansell.

BRAZIL 1992 WILLIAMS-RENAULT
Victory and pole position for Mansell. Fastest lap for Patrese.

SPAIN 1992 WILLIAMS-RENAULT
Pole position, victory and fastest lap for Mansell.

SAN MARINO 1992 WILLIAMS-RENAULT
Pole position, victory and fastest lap for Mansell.

FRANCE 1992 WILLIAMS-RENAULT
Pole position, victory and fastest lap for Mansell.

GREAT BRITAIN 1992 WILLIAMS-RENAULT
Pole position, victory and fastest lap for Mansell.

GERMANY 1992 WILLIAMS-RENAULT
Victory and pole position for Mansell. Fastest lap for Patrese.

JAPAN 1992 WILLIAMS-RENAULT
Victory for Patrese. Pole position and fastest lap for Mansell.

SOUTH AFRICA 1993 WILLIAMS-RENAULT
Pole position, victory and fastest lap for Prost.

SAN MARINO 1993 WILLIAMS-RENAULT
Pole position, victory and fastest lap for Prost.

GREAT BRITAIN 1993 WILLIAMS-RENAULT
Victory and pole position for Prost. Fastest lap for Hill.

BELGIUM 1993 WILLIAMS-RENAULT
Victory for Hill. Pole position and fastest lap for Prost.

ITALY 1993 WILLIAMS-RENAULT
Victory and fastest lap for Hill. Pole position for Prost.

GREAT BRITAIN 1994 WILLIAMS-RENAULT
Pole position, victory and fastest lap for Hill.

ARGENTINA 1995
Victory for Hill (Williams-Renault). Pole position for Coulthard (Williams-Renault). Fastest lap for Schumacher (Benetton-Renault).

SPAIN 1995
Victory and pole position for Schumacher (Benetton-Renault). Fastest lap for Hill (Williams-Renault).

FRANCE 1995
Victory and fastest lap for Schumacher (Benetton-Renault). Pole position for Hill (Williams-Renault).

GREAT BRITAIN 1995
Victory for Herbert (Benetton-Renault). Pole position and fastest lap for Hill (Williams-Renault).

GERMANY 1995
Victory and fastest lap for Schumacher (Benetton-Renault). Pole position for Hill (Williams-Renault).

HUNGARY 1995
Pole position, victory and fastest lap for Hill (Williams-Renault).

PORTUGAL 1995
Pole position, victory and fastest lap for Coulthard (Williams-Renault).

EUROPE 1995
Victory and fastest lap for Schumacher (Benetton-Renault). Pole position for Coulthard (Williams-Renault).

PACIFIC 1995
Victory and fastest lap for Schumacher (Benetton-Renault). Pole position for Coulthard (Williams-Renault).

JAPAN 1995
Pole position, victory and fastest lap for Schumacher (Benetton-Renault).

AUSTRALIA 1995
Pole position, victory and fastest lap for Hill (Williams-Renault).

AUSTRALIA 1996
Victory for Hill (Williams-Renault). Pole position and fastest lap for Villeneuve (Williams-Renault).

BRAZIL 1996
Pole position, victory and fastest lap for Hill (Williams-Renault).

ARGENTINA 1996
Victory and pole position for Hill (Williams-Renault). Fastest lap for Alesi (Benetton Renault).

EUROPE 1996
Victory for Villeneuve (Williams-Renault). Pole position and fastest lap for Hill (Williams-Renault).

CANADA 1996
Victory and pole position for Hill (Williams-Renault). Fastest lap for Villeneuve (Williams-Renault).

GREAT BRITAIN 1996
Victory and fastest lap for Villeneuve (Williams-Renault). Pole position for Hill (Williams-Renault).

GERMANY 1996
Pole position, victory and fastest lap for Hill (Williams-Renault).

PORTUGAL 1996
Victory and fastest lap for Villeneuve (Williams-Renault). Pole position for Hill (Williams-Renault).

JAPAN 1996
Victory for Hill (Williams-Renault). Pole position and fastest lap for Villeneuve (Williams-Renault).

BRAZIL 1997
Pole position, victory and fastest lap for Villeneuve (Williams-Renault).

ARGENTINA 1997
Victory and pole position for Villeneuve (Williams-Renault). Fastest lap for Berger (Benetton-Renault).

SAN MARINO 1997
Victory and fastest lap for Frentzen (Williams-Renault). Pole position for Villeneuve (Williams-Renault).

GERMANY 1997
Pole position, victory and fastest lap for Berger (Benetton-Renault).

AUSTRIA 1997
Pole position, victory and fastest lap for Villeneuve (Williams-Renault).

**Patrick Tambay,
South African GP,
7 April 1984**

'GRAND SLAMS' WITH RENAULT POWER

(Grand Slam: Triple Crown plus race led from start to finish)

1980 Brazil and South Africa
1982 South Africa
1985 Portugal
1990 Hungary
1991 Mexico, Great Britain, Portugal
1992 South Africa, Brazil, Spain, San Marino, France, Great Britain, Germany and Japan
1993 Hungary
1995 Spain, France, Great Britain, Germany, Hungary, Portugal, Pacific and Australia
1996 Australia, Brazil, Argentina, Europe, Canada, Great Britain, Germany, Portugal and Japan

RENAULT 1-2s

France 1982 1 Arnoux; 2 Prost (Both Renault)
USA 1986 1 Senna (Lotus-Renault); 2 Lafitte (Ligier-Renault)
Canada 1989 1 Boutsen; 2 Patrese (Both Williams-Renault)
Mexico 1991 1 Patrese; Mansell (Both Williams-Renault)
Germany 1991 1 Mansell; 2 Patrese (Both Williams-Renault)
South Africa 1992 1 Mansell; 2 Patrese (Both Williams-Renault)
Mexico 1992 1 Mansell; 2 Patrese (Both Williams-Renault)
Brazil 1992 1 Mansell; 2 Patrese (Both Williams-Renault)
San Marino 1992 1 Mansell; 2 Patrese (Both Williams-Renault)
France 1992 1 Mansell; 2 Patrese (Both Williams-Renault)

Great Britain 1992 1 Mansell; 2 Patrese (Both Williams-Renault)
France 1993 1 Prost; 2 Hill (Both Williams-Renault)
Portugal 1994 1 Hill; 2 Coulthard (Both Williams-Renault)
Brazil 1995 1 Schumacher (Benetton-Renault); 2 Coulthard (Williams-Renault)
Spain 1995 1 Schumacher; 2 Herbert (Both Benetton-Renault)
Monaco 1995 1 Schumacher (Benetton-Renault); 2 Hill (Williams-Renault)
France 1995 1 Schumacher (Benetton-Renault); 2 Hill (Williams-Renault)
Germany 1995 1Schumacher (Benetton-Renault); 2 Coulthard (Williams-Renault)
Hungary 1995 1 Hill; 2 Coulthard (Both Williams-Renault)
Belgium 1995 1 Schumacher (Benetton-Renault); 2 Hill (Williams-Renault)
Portugal 1995 1 Coulthard (Williams-Renault); 2 Schumacher (Benetton-Renault)
Pacific 1995 Schumacher (Benetton-Renault); 2 Coulthard (Williams-Renault)
Australia 1996 1 Hill; 2 Villeneuve (Both Williams-Renault)
Brazil 1996 1 Hill (Williams-Renault); 2 Alesi (Benetton-Renault)
Argentina 1996 1 Hill; 2 Villeneuve (Both Williams-Renault)
Canada 1996 1 Hill; 2 Villeneuve (Both Williams-Renault)
France 1996 1 Hill; 2 Villeneuve (Both Williams-Renault)
Great Britain 1996 1 Villeneuve (Williams-Renault); 2 Berger (Benetton-Renault)
Germany 1996 1 Hill (Williams-Renault); 2 Alesi (Benetton-Renault)
Hungary 1996 1 Villeneuve; 2 Hill (Both Williams-Renault)
Portugal 1996 1 Villeneuve; 2 Hill (Both Williams-Renault)
Brazil 1997 1 Villeneuve (Williams-Renault); 2 Berger (Benetton-Renault)
Great Britain 1997 1 Villeneuve (Williams-Renault); 2 Alesi (Benetton-Renault)
Luxembourg 1997 1 Villeneuve (Williams-Renault); 2 Alesi (Benetton-Renault)

ALL-RENAULT FRONT ROWS

France 1979 Jabouille and Arnoux (Both Renault)
Italy 1979 Jabouille and Arnoux (Both Renault)
South Africa 1980 Jabouille and Arnoux (Both Renault)
Austria 1980 Arnoux and Jabouille (Both Renault)
Holland 1980 Arnoux and Jabouille (Both Renault)
Italy 1980 Arnoux and Jabouille (Both Renault)
Great Britain 1981 Arnoux and Prost (Both Renault)
Germany 1981 Prost and Arnoux (Both Renault)
Austria 1981 Arnoux and Prost (Both Renault)
Holland 1981 Prost and Arnoux (Both Renault)
San Marino 1982 Arnoux and Prost (Both Renault)
Belgium 1982 Prost and Arnoux (Both Renault)
Holland 1982 Arnoux and Prost (Both Renault)
France 1982 Arnoux and Prost (Both Renault)
Switzerland 1982 Prost and Arnoux (Both Renault)
USA 1982 Prost and Arnoux (Both Renault)
France 1983 Prost and Cheever (Both Renault)
France 1984 Tambay (Renault) and De Angelis (Lotus-Renault)
USA 1984 Mansell and De Angelis (Both Lotus-Renault)
Canada 1985 De Angelis and Senna (Both Lotus-Renault)
Hungary 1990 Boutsen and Patrese (Both Williams-Renault)
Canada 1991 Patrese and Mansell (Both Williams-Renault)
Mexico 1991 Patrese and Mansell (Both Williams-Renault)
Mexico 1992 Mansell and Patrese (Both Williams-Renault)
Brazil 1992 Mansell and Patrese (Both Williams-Renault)
San Marino 1992 Mansell and Patrese (Both Williams-Renault)
France 1992 Mansell and Patrese (Both Williams-Renault)

Great Britain 1992 Mansell and Patrese (Both Williams-Renault)
Germany 1992 Mansell and Patrese (Both Williams-Renault)
Hungary 1992 Patrese and Mansell (Both Williams-Renault)
Portugal 1992 Mansell and Patrese (Both Williams-Renault)
Japan 1992 Mansell and Patrese (Both Williams-Renault)
Brazil 1993 Prost and Hill (Both Williams-Renault)
Europe 1993 Prost and Hill (Both Williams-Renault)
San Marino 1993 Prost and Hill (Both Williams-Renault)
Spain 1993 Prost and Hill (Both Williams-Renault)
Canada 1993 Prost and Hill (Both Williams-Renault)
France 1993 Hill and Prost (Both Williams-Renault)
Great Britain 1993 Prost and Hill (Both Williams-Renault)
Germany 1993 Prost and Hill (Both Williams-Renault)
Hungary 1993 Prost and Hill (Both Williams-Renault)
Belgium 1993 Prost and Hill (Both Williams-Renault)
Italy 1993 Prost and Hill (Both Williams-Renault)
Portugal 1993 Hill and Prost (Both Williams-Renault)
France 1994 Hill and Mansell (Both Williams-Renault)
Brazil 1995 Hill (Williams-Renault) and Schumacher (Benetton-Renault)
Argentina 1995 Coulthard and Hill (Both Williams-Renault)
Monaco 1995 Hill (Williams-Renault) and Schumacher (Benetton-Renault)
Canada 1995 Schumacher (Benetton-Renault) and Hill (Williams-Renault)
France 1995 Hill (Williams-Renault) and Schumacher (Benetton-Renault)
Great Britain 1995 Hill and Coulthard (Both Williams-Renault)
Germany 1995 Hill (Williams-Renault) and Schumacher (Benetton-Renault)

South African GP, 3 March 1979

Hungary 1995 Hill and Coulthard (Both Williams-Renault)
Italy 1995 Coulthard (Williams-Renault) and Schumacher (Benetton-Renault)
Portugal 1995 Coulthard and Hill (Both Williams-Renault)
Europe 1995 Coulthard and Hill (Both Williams-Renault)
Pacific 1995 Coulthard and Hill (Both Williams-Renault)
Australia 1995 Hill and Coulthard (Both Williams-Renault)
Australia 1996 Villeneuve and Hill (Both Williams-Renault)
Europe 1996 Hill and Villeneuve (Both Williams-Renault)
Spain 1996 Hill and Villeneuve (Both Williams-Renault)
Canada 1996 Hill and Villeneuve (Both Williams-Renault)
Great Britain 1996 Hill and Villeneuve (Both Williams-Renault)
Germany 1996 Hill (Williams-Renault) and Berger (Benetton-Renault)
Belgium 1996 Villeneuve and Hill (Both Williams-Renault)
Italy 1996 Hill and Villeneuve (Both Williams-Renault)
Portugal 1996 Hill and Villeneuve (Both Williams-Renault)
Japan 1996 Villeneuve and Hill (Both Williams-Renault)
Australia 1997 Villeneuve and Frentzen (Both Williams-Renault)
Argentina 1997 Villeneuve and Frentzen (Both Williams-Renault)
San Marino 1997 Villeneuve and Frentzen (Both Williams-Renault)
Spain 1997 Villeneuve and Frentzen (Both Williams-Renault)
Great Britain 1997 Villeneuve and Frentzen (Both Williams-Renault)
Belgium 1997 Villeneuve (Williams-Renault) and Alesi (Benetton-Renault)
Italy 1997 Alesi (Benetton-Renault) and Frentzen (Williams-Renault)

NUMBER OF ALL-RENAULT FRONT ROWS BY PAIRS OF DRIVERS:

12: Prost-Hill, Mansell-Patrese
10: Prost-Arnoux
9: Villeneuve-Hill
6: Jabouille-Arnoux, Schumacher-Hill
5: Villeneuve-Frentzen, Hill-Coulthard
1: Prost-Cheever, Tambay-De Angelis, Mansell-De Angelis, De Angelis-Senna, Boutsen-Patrese, Hill-Mansell, Coulthard-Schumacher, Hill-Berger, Villeneuve-Alesi, Alesi-Frentzen

16 'ABSOLUTE DOMINATIONS' WITH RENAULT POWER

('Absolute Domination': All Renault-powered front row; race led from start to finish, one-two result and fastest lap)

1991 Mexico
1992 South Africa, Brazil, San Marino, France, Great Britain
1995 France, Germany, Hungary, Portugal, Pacific
1996 Australia, Canada, Great Britain, Germany, Portugal

FOUR RENAULT ENGINES ON THE FIRST TWO ROWS OF THE GRID

France 1993: 1 Hill (Williams-Renault), 2 Prost (Williams-Renault), 3 Brundle (Ligier-Renault), 4 Blundell (Ligier-Renault)
Brazil 1995: 1 Hill (Williams-Renault); 2 Schumacher (Benetton-Renault), 3 Coulthard (Williams-Renault), 4 Herbert (Benetton-Renault)

Brazilian GP, 25 March 1990.

RENAULT ENGINES IN THE POINTS

FOUR RENAULT ENGINES IN THE POINTS (NUMBERS REFER TO RACE POSITIONS)

MONACO 1985
3 De Angelis (Lotus-Renault)
4 De Cesaris (Ligier-Renault)
5 Warwick (Renault)
6 Lafitte (Ligier-Renault)

BRAZIL 1986
2 Senna (Lotus-Renault)
3 Lafitte (Ligier-Renault)
4 Arnoux (Ligier-Renault)
5 Brundle (Tyrell-Renault)

PACIFIC 1995
1 Schumacher (Benetton-Renault)
2 Coulthard (Williams-Renault)
3 Hill (Williams-Renault)
6 Herbert (Benetton-Renault)

FRANCE 1996
1 Hill (Williams-Renault)
2 Villeneuve (Williams-Renault)
3 Alesi (Benetton-Renault)
4 Berger (Benetton-Renault)

BELGIUM 1996
2 Villeneuve (Williams-Renault)
4 Alesi (Benetton-Renault)
5 Hill (Williams-Renault)
6 Berger (Benetton-Renault)

PORTUGAL 1996
1 Villeneuve (Williams-Renault)
2 Hill (Williams-Renault)
4 Alesi (Benetton-Renault)
6 Berger (Benetton-Renault)

LUXEMBOURG 1997
1 Villeneuve (Williams-Renault)
2 Alesi (Benetton-Renault)
3 Frentzen (Williams-Renault)
4 Berger (Benetton-Renault)

THREE RENAULT ENGINES IN THE POINTS IN ONE RACE:

SAN MARINO 1984
3 De Angelis (Lotus-Renault)
4 Warwick (Renault)
6 De Cesaris (Ligier-Renault)

FRANCE 1984
2 Tambay (Renault)
3 Mansell (Lotus-Renault)
5 De Angelis (Lotus-Renault)

GERMANY 1984
3 Warwick (Renault)
4 Mansell (Lotus-Renault)
5 Tambay (Renault)

HOLLAND 1984
3 Mansell (Lotus-Renault)
4 De Angelis (Lotus-Renault)
5 Tambay (Renault)

BRAZIL 1985
3 De Angelis (Lotus-Renault)
5 Tambay (Renault)
6 Lafitte (Ligier-Renault)

PORTUGAL 1985
1 Senna (Lotus-Renault)
3 Tambay (Renault)
4 De Angelis (Lotus-Renault)

AUSTRALIA 1985
2 Lafitte (Ligier-Renault)
3 Streiff (Ligier-Renault)
4 Capelli (Tyrrell-Renault)

MONACO 1986
3 Senna (Lotus-Renault)
5 Arnoux (Ligier-Renault)
6 Lafitte (Ligier-Renault)

GREAT BRITAIN 1986
4 Arnoux (Ligier-Renault)
5 Brundle (Tyrrell-Renault)
6 Streiff (Tyrrell-Renault)

HUNGARY 1986
2 Senna (Lotus-Renault)
5 Dumfries (Lotus-Renault)
6 Brundle (Tyrrell-Renault)

AUSTRALIA 1986
4 Brundle (Tyrrell-Renault)
5 Streiff (Tyrrell-Renault)
6 Dumfries (Lotus-Renault)

FRANCE 1992
1 Mansell (Williams-Renault)
2 Patrese (Williams-Renault)
5 Comas (Ligier-Renault)

MONACO 1993
2 Hill (Williams-Renault)
4 Prost (Williams-Renault)
6 Brundle (Ligier-Renault)

CANADA 1993
1 Prost (Williams-Renault)
3 Hill (Williams-Renault)
5 Brundle (Ligier-Renault)

FRANCE 1993
1 Prost (Williams-Renault)
2 Hill (Williams-Renault)
5 Brundle (Ligier-Renault)

PORTUGAL 1993
2 Prost (Williams-Renault)
3 Hill (Williams-Renault)
6 Brundle (Ligier-Renault)

AUSTRALIA 1993
2 Prost (Williams-Renault)
3 Hill (Williams-Renault)
6 Brundle (Ligier-Renault)

ARGENTINA 1995
1 Hill (Williams-Renault)
3 Schumacher (Benetton-Renault)
4 Herbert (Benetton-Renault)

SPAIN 1995
1 Schumacher (Benetton-Renault)
2 Herbert (Benetton-Renault)
4 Hill (Williams-Renault)

MONACO 1995
1 Schumacher (Benetton-Renault)
2 Hill (Williams-Renault)
4 Herbert (Benetton-Renault)

FRANCE 1995
1 Schumacher (Benetton-Renault)
2 Hill (Williams-Renault)
3 Coulthard (Williams-Renault)

GERMANY 1995
1 Schumacher (Benetton-Renault)
2 Coulthard (Williams-Renault)
4 Herbert (Benetton-Renault)

HUNGARY 1995
1 Hill (Williams-Renault)
2 Coulthard (Williams-Renault)
4 Herbert (Benetton-Renault)

PORTUGAL 1995
1 Coulthard (Williams-Renault)
2 Schumacher (Benetton-Renault)
3 Hill (Williams-Renault)

EUROPE 1995
1 Schumacher (Benetton-Renault)
2 Coulthard (Williams-Renault)
4 Herbert (Benetton-Renault)

AUSTRALIA 1996
1 Hill (Williams-Renault)
2 Villeneuve (Williams-Renault)
4 Berger (Benetton-Renault)

ARGENTINA 1996
1 Hill (Williams-Renault)
2 Villeneuve (Williams-Renault)
3 Alesi (Benetton-Renault)

SAN MARINO 1996
1 Hill (Williams-Renault)
3 Berger (Benetton-Renault)
6 Alesi (Benetton-Renault)

GERMANY 1996
1 Hill (Williams-Renault)
2 Alesi (Benetton-Renault)
3 Villeneuve (Williams-Renault)

HUNGARY 1996
1 Villeneuve (Williams-Renault)
2 Hill (Williams-Renault)
3 Alesi (Benetton-Renault)

BRAZIL 1997
1 Villeneuve (Williams-Renault)
2 Berger (Benetton-Renault)
6 Alesi (Benetton-Renault)

FRANCE 1997
2 Frentzen (Williams-Renault)
4 Villeneuve (Williams-Renault)
5 Alesi (Benetton-Renault)

GREAT BRITAIN 1997
1 Villeneuve (Williams-Renault)
2 Alesi (Benetton-Renault)
3 Wurz (Benetton-Renault)

BELGIUM 1997
3 Frentzen (Williams-Renault)
5 Villeneuve (Williams-Renault)
6 Berger (Benetton-Renault)

ITALY 1997
2 Alesi (Benetton-Renault)
3 Frentzen (Williams-Renault)
5 Villeneuve (Williams-Renault)

133

DRIVERS' WORLD CHAMPIONSHIP

1978
Jean-Pierre Jabouille Renault 3pts 17th

1979
Rene Arnoux Renault 17pts 8th
Jean-Pierre Jabouille Renault 9pts 13th

1980
Rene Arnoux Renault 29pts 6th
Jean-Pierre Jabouille Renault 9pts 8th

1981
Alain Prost Renault 43pts 5th
Rene Arnoux Renault 11pts 9th

1982
Alain Prost Renault 34pts 4th
Rene Arnoux 28pts 6th

1983
Alain Prost Renault 57pts 2nd
Eddie Cheever Renault 22pts 6th
Nigel Mansell Lotus-Renault 10pts 13th
Elio De Angelis Lotus-Renault 2pts 17th

1984
Elio De Angelis Lotus-Renault 34pts 3rd
Derek Warwick Renault 23pts 7th
Nigel Mansell Lotus-Renault 13pts 9th
Patrick Tambay Renault 11pts 11th
Andrea De Cesaris Ligier-Renault 3pts 17th

1985
Ayrton Senna Lotus-Renault 38pts 4th
Elio De Angelis Lotus-Renault 3pts 5th
Jacques Lafitte Ligier-Renault 16pts 9th
Patrick Tambay Renault 11pts 12th
Derek Warwick Renault 5pts 14th
Stefan Bellof Tyrell-Renault 4pts 15th
Philippe Streiff Ligier-Renault 4pts 15th
Ivan Capelli Tyrell-Renault 3pts 19th
Andrea De Cesaris Ligier-Renault 3pts 19th

1986
Ayrton Senna Lotus-Renault 55pts 4th
Rene Arnoux Ligier-Renault 14pts 9th
Jacques Lafitte Ligier-Renault 14pts 9th
Martin Brundle Tyrrell-Renault 5pts 11th
Johnny Dumfries Lotus-Renault 3pts 13th
Philippe Streiff Tyrell-Renault 3pts 13th
Philippe Alliot Ligier-Renault 1pt 19th

1989
Riccardo Patrese Williams-Renault 40pts 3rd
Thierry Boutsen Williams-Renault 37pts 5th

1990
Thierry Boutsen Williams-Renault 34pts 6th
Riccardo Patrese Williams-Renault 23pts 7th

1991
Nigel Mansell Williams-Renault 72pts 2nd
Riccardo Patrese Williams-Renault 53pts 3rd

1992
Nigel Mansell Williams-Renault 108pts 1st
Riccardo Patrese Williams-Renault 86pts 2nd
Erik Comas Ligier-Renault 4pts 11th
Thierry Boutsen Ligier-Renault 2pts 14th

1993
Alain Prost Williams-Renault 99pts 1st
Damon Hill Williams-Renault 69pts 3rd
Martin Brundle Ligier-Renault 13pts 7th
Mark Blundell Ligier-Renault 10pts 10th

1994
Damon Hill Williams-Renault 91pts 2nd
David Coulthard Williams-Renault 14pts 8th
Nigel Mansell Williams-Renault 13pts 9th
Olivier Panis Ligier-Renault 9pts 11th
Eric Barnard Ligier-Renault 4pts 18th

1995
Michael Schumacher Benetton-Renault 102pts 1st
Damon Hill Williams-Renault 69pts 2nd
David Coulthard Williams-Renault 49pts 3rd
Johnny Herbert Benetton-Renault 45pts 4th

1996
Damon Hill Williams-Renault 97pts 1st

Jacques Villeneuve Williams-Renault 78pts 2nd
Jean Alesi Benetton-Renault 47pts 4th
Gerhard Berger Benetton-Renault 21pts 6th

1997
Jacques Villeneuve Williams-Renault 81pts 1st
Heinz-Harald Frentzen Williams-Renault 42pts 3rd
Jean Alesi Benetton-Renault 36pts 4th
Gerhard Berger Benetton-Renault 27pts 6th
Alexander Wurz Benetton-Renault 4pts 15th

CONSTRUCTORS' CHAMPIONSHIP

1978
Renault EF1 V6 3pts 13th

1979
Renault EF1 V6 26pts 6th

1980
Renault EF1 V6 38pts 4th

1981
Renault EF1 V6 54pts 3rd

1982
Renault EF1 V6 62pts 3rd

1983
Renault EF1 V6 79pts 2nd
Lotus-Renault EF1/EF48 V6 11pts 8th

1984
Lotus-Renault EF48 V6 47pts 3rd
Renault EF4 V6 34pts 5th
Ligier-Renault EF4 V6 3pts 12th

1985
Lotus-Renault EF48/EF15 V6 71pts 3rd
Ligier-Renault EF48/EF15 V6 23pts 6th
Renault EF48 V6 12pts 8th
Renault EF15 V6 4pts 9th
Tyrrell-Renault EF48/EF15 V6 3pts 11th

1986
Lotus-Renault EF15B V6 58pts 3rd
Ligier-Renault EF48/EF15 V6 29pts 5th
Tyrrell-Renault EF48/EF15 V6 11pts 7th

1989
Williams-Renault RS1 V10 77pts 2nd

1990
Williams-Renault RS2 V10 57pts 4th

1991
Williams-Renault RS3 V10 l25pts 2nd

1992
Williams-Renault RS3 V10 164pts 1st
Ligier-Renault RS3 V10 6pts 9th

1993
Williams-Renault RS5 V10 168pts 1st
Ligier-Renault RS5 V10 23pts 5th

1994
Williams-Renault RS6 V10 118pts 1st
Ligier-Renault RS5 V10 13pts 6th

1995
Benetton-Renault RS7 V10 147pts 1st
Williams RS7 V10 118pts 2nd

1996
Williams-Renault RS8B V10 175pts 1st
Benetton-Renault RS8B V10 68pts 3rd

1997
Williams-Renault RS9B V10 123pts 1st
Benetton-Renault RS9B V10 67pts 3rd

**Podium, San Marino GP,
31 May 1990**

Mansell and Patrese, German GP, 28 July 1991

The Renault Engines:
Nine Seasons Nine Engines

Pioneer of the turbo engines, Renault withdrew from Formula One at the end of 1986 to come back two years later with a new generation of normally aspirated V10 engines, the first of which was named RS1.

The series evolved until the RS9, enabling Williams-Renault to win the F1 Constructors' World Championship title in 1992 with the RS4, in 1993 with the RS5, in 1994 with the RS6, in 1996 with the RS8 and in 1997 with the RS9. Benetton-Renault meanwhile won the Constructors' World Championship title in 1995 with the RS7 engine.

Nine years, nine engines – and nine challenges.

RENAULT RS1 ENGINE

16 Grand Prix in 1989
2 wins: Canada and Australia
1 pole position: Hungary
1 fastest lap: Brazil
77 points scored
2nd in the Constructors' World Championship with Williams.

Main characteristics:
Type: V10 (The V forming an angle of 67 degrees)
Length: 668mm
Width: 550mm
Height (to cylinder heads): 440mm
Weight: 141kg
Cylinder block and heads in aluminium; sump and timing housing in light aluminium
Four valves per cylinder
Pneumatic timing
Magneti-Marelli central electronic engine management and static ignition

Bernard Dudot: 'The Renault RS1 was an "all-round" engine. So much so that, at the time of its design, we did not know which team – and therefore which chassis – it would power. As a consequence we based our thinking on the general view that a modern F1 engine must form an integral part of a Formula One car's chassis. We consulted a number of chassis engineers about what they thought to be the

best type of power unit for Formula One: V8, V10, V12. In each case we also indicated what we thought would be the approximate sizes of the engines in question, as well as their anticipated performance and fuel consumption. Their choice was a V10 with a small-angled V. It wasn't the easiest option for us to produce but we had the advantage of being able to take our time because Renault had suspended its direct involvement in Formula One at the time.

This engine was bench tested for the first time in January 1988, one year later than Honda's normally aspirated engine. Despite this initial delay it proved successful when raced, a feat due in part to two technical innovations that have tended to become widely used since: pneumatic timing and static ignition with one capacitor per cylinder. For its maiden race in Brazil, Riccardo Patrese put the RS1 engine on the front row of the grid and set the fastest lap. By the end of the season it had scored two wins and finished the year as runner-up in the Constructors' World Championship. It had achieved its objective.'

RENAULT RS2 ENGINE

16 Grand Prix in 1990
2 wins: San Marino and Hungary
1 pole position: Hungary
5 fastest laps: Germany, Hungary, Portugal, Spain, Japan.
57 points scored
4th in the Constructors' World Championship with Williams

Main characteristics:
Type: V10 (67 degrees)
Length: 620mm
Width: 550mm
Height (to cylinder heads): 425mm
Weight: 139kg
Cylinder block and heads in aluminium; sump and timing housing in light aluminium
Four valves per cylinder
Pneumatic timing
Magneti-Marelli central electronic engine management and static ignition

Changes compared to the RS1:
Distribution and pump control using a cascade of gears instead of synchronous belts
A shortening of the engine length by 48mm
A lowering of the engine top by 15mm
Complete redefinition of induction

Bernard Dudot: 'The main difference compared with the RS1 was that it was designed as a function of a known chassis in close collaboration with engineers from Williams. With the RS2, we had solved the basic shortcomings revealed by the RS1. The new engine was slightly shorter than the RS1. More rigid at the front, it featured a new head design and a revised layout of the oil and water circuits to suit the specifics of the Williams, something we hadn't been able to do with the RS1 simply because we hadn't known which chassis it would eventually power. We had expected a great deal from the RS2, but it was never able to compensate for the problems thrown up that year by the Williams chassis. As in 1989, we won two races and set a number of fastest laps, but we also slipped two places in the Constructors' World Championship.'

RENAULT RS3 ENGINE

26 Grand Prix – 16 in 1991 and 10 in 1992
15 wins:
1991: Mexico, France, Great Britain, Germany, Italy, Portugal and Spain
1992: South Africa, Mexico, Brazil, San Marino, France, Great Britain and Germany
14 pole positions:
1991: Canada, Mexico, France, Great Britain, Germany and Portugal
1992: South Africa, Mexico, Brazil, Spain, San Marino, Monaco, France and Great Britain
16 fastest laps:
1991: Brazil, Canada, Mexico, Great Britain, Germany, Portugal and Spain
1992: South Africa, Brazil, Spain, San Marino, Monaco, France, Great Britain and Germany
251 points scored: 125 in 1991 and 126 in 1992
2nd in the 1991 Constructors' World

Championship with Williams
1st in the 1992 Constructors' World Championship with Williams

Main characteristics:
Type: V10 (67 degrees)
Length: 620mm
Width: 550mm
Height (to cylinder head): 411mm
Weight: 137kg
Cylinder block and heads in aluminium; sump and timing housing in light aluminium
Four valves per cylinder
Pneumatic timing
Magneti-Marelli central electronic engine management and static ignition

Changes compared to the RS2:
New bore and stroke valves
Complete redefinition of upper part of engine in particular
A new cylinder head
New drive of camshafts
New induction
Stiffening of the distribution front
New lower sump with rearranged oil-drain circulation
New, much more powerful, Magneti-Marelli electronic management unit – significantly smaller in terms of weight and volume
Reduction in height of 14mm

Bernard Dudot: 'Apart from its track record, I will always remember the Renault RS3 for its reliability. In twenty-six Grand Prix with Williams, it was not once the cause of a single retirement. Compared with the RS2, the RS3 had a new bore and stroke, a new oil-draining system, a new head and distribution chamber design. Its career turned out to be longer than expected. In agreement with Frank Williams, we decided to start the 1992 season with a new version of the engine, the RS3C. In 1991 our chassis-engine package had been the best in Formula One but we missed out on the title because of a lack of reliability at the start of the season when we scored just twelve points from the first four Grand Prix compared with forty-nine for McLaren. For 1992 Williams introduced a major innovation in the form of reactive suspension.

In light of the preceding season, we decided to limit the technical risk factor and start the year with a known entity insofar as the engine was concerned. Initially the RS3C was designed as a function of the two high-altitude circuits scheduled for the start of the season but the results were so successful that the Renault RS3C was used right up to the German Grand Prix – which it won.'

RENAULT RS4 ENGINE

This was the engine that powered the Williams-Renault when Nigel Mansell clinched the 1992 drivers' crown in Hungary and when Williams-Renault secured the 1992 Constructors' World Championship' title in Belgium.

6 Grand Prix in 1992:
(Replaced the Renault RS3 as from Hungary, but was first used in qualifying in Spain, San Marino, Canada, France, Great Britain and Germany.)
2 wins: Portugal and Japan
7 pole positions: Germany, Hungary, Belgium, Italy, Portugal, Japan and Australia
38 points scored

Main characteristics:
Type: V10 (67 degrees)
Length: 620mm
Width: 550mm
Height (to cylinder heads): 411mm
Weight: 137kg
Cylinder block and heads in aluminium; sump and timing housing in light aluminium
Four valves per cylinder
Pneumatic timing
Magneti-Marelli central electronic engine management and static ignition

Changes compared to the RS3:
Compared with the RS3, the RS4 is basically differentiated by a cylinder head that made it possible to put in place a new distribution control unit. It also had a new bore/stroke ratio.

Bernard Dudot: 'The Renault RS4 made its maiden appearance in qualifying for the fourth Grand Prix of 1992, Spain, before making its race debut three months and seven Grand Prix later in Hungary. As far as performance is concerned the RS4 marks an important step forward compared to the RS3. Bore and stroke are different and the timing system is new. Having used it in practice, the Williams drivers naturally wanted to race it as soon as possible. That was understandable. A driver always wants to have the best car and engine at his disposal. However, we didn't want to make the switch too quickly. We had total confidence in the RS3, which continued to give full satisfaction as far as performance was concerned. The Renault RS4 eventually made its debut in Hungary and, on its first race, it helped clinch the drivers' title for Nigel Mansell. For its second race, in Belgium, it took Williams and Renault to the Constructors' World Championship title. Since its debut, the RS4 has given Williams pole position at each Grand Prix.'

RENAULT RS5 ENGINE

This engine powered the Williams-Renault throughout the 1993 season, taking Alain Prost to the Drivers' World Championship at the Portuguese Grand Prix and Williams-Renault to the constructors' crown at the Belgian Grand Prix.

16 Grand Prix:
10 wins: South Africa, San Marino, Spain, Canada, France, Great Britain, Germany, Hungary, Belgium and Italy
15 pole positions: South Africa, Brazil, Europe, San Marino, Spain, Monaco, Canada, France, Great Britain, Germany, Hungary, Belgium, Italy, Portugal and Japan
10 fastest laps: South Africa, San Marino, Monaco, Great Britain, Hungary, Belgium, Italy, Portugal, Japan and Australia.
168 points scored

Main characteristics:
Type: V10 (67 degrees)
Length: 620mm
Width: 550mm
Height (to cylinder head): 411mm
Weight: 137kg
Cylinder block and heads in aluminium; sump and timing housing in light aluminium
Four valves per cylinder
Pneumatic timing
Magneti-Marelli central electronic engine management and static ignition

Changes compared to the RS4:
The entire upper part of the engine had been redesigned for:
Inlet design
Combustion chambers
Timing
The lower part of the engine for:
New con-rod design

Bernard Dudot: 'The RS5 was closely derived from the RS4, which had only served for the final six Grand Prix of the 1992 season. While fate had it that 1993 was marked with three engine-related driver retirements with Williams (including Alain Prost at Monza, which resulted in putting off his fourth World title until Estoril two weeks later) the RS5 proved very reliable on the whole, with no problems encountered in official practice with either Williams or Ligier and no race problems to report with Ligier.

Throughout the 1993 season, the RS5 engine evolved constantly, in small steps from one Grand Prix to another, with no major evolutions. For Canada, a new electronically controlled throttle was introduced that marked a considerable improvement as far as ease of use and driveability were concerned.

A significant step forward was made towards the end of the year with the introduction of a new timing system. However, since the reliability of this system was not judged sufficient for races, it was only used for practice.'

RENAULT RS6 ENGINE

The Renault RS6, which powered both the Williams and Ligier cars throughout the 1994 season, took Williams to a further title in the Formula One Constructors' World Championship.

RS6:
8 Grand Prix: Brazil, Pacific, San Marino, Spain, Canada, France and Great Britain.
2 wins: France and Great Britain
5 pole positions: Brazil, Pacific, San Marino, France and Great Britain
2 fastest laps: France and Great Britain
43 points scored

RS6B:
6 Grand Prix: Germany, Hungary, Belgium, Italy, Portugal and Europe
3 wins: Belgium, Italy and Portugal
4 fastest laps: Germany, Belgium, Italy and Portugal
52 points scored

RS6C:
2 Grand Prix: Japan and Australia
2 wins
1 pole position: Australia
1 fastest lap: Japan
23 points scored

Main characteristics:
Type: V10 (67 degrees)
Length: 623mm
Width: 550mm
Height (to cylinder heads): 413mm
Weight: 134/136kg according to accessories
Aluminium cylinders; light aluminium crankcase, sump and timing housing
Four valves per cylinder
Pneumatic timing
Magneti-Marelli central electronic engine management and static ignition

Changes compared to the RS5:
The entire top end of the engine had been redesigned for:
Intake and exhaust

Combustion chambers
Timing
The bottom end modification:
New moving parts

Bernard Dudot: 'The RS6 arose from the requirement to use a single engine for both qualifying and races in 1994 as initially planned in the regulations drawn up at the beginning of 1993. When this idea was dropped and the decision taken to continue into 1994 on the basis of the 1993 regulations, we had already gone a long way down the road of developing a reliable base from which we were consequently able to work. As a result of the decision to revert to 1993 rules we revised the top end, redesigned the cylinder heads (combustion chambers, inlet and outlet ports) and modified the timing system to achieve an improvement of around 3,400rpm in maximum revs compared with the previous year. The bottom end was also revised in order to cope with the constraints resulting from this increase in engine speed. Finally, with a view of reducing the aerodynamic drag of the chassis, a special effort was made to improve the engine's thermal properties. One of the outstanding features of the RS6 engine was reliability. If you count both the Williams and Ligier teams, from a total of sixty-three Grand Prix starts not a single race retirement was due to an engine problem in the course of 1994, the best score to date for a Renault Formula One engine.

The engine evolved considerably in the course of the season thanks notably to a new version of the air valves and a new timing drive system – the highly sophisticated design of which allowed us to eliminate a vibration in the system. Williams used a revised RS6B version in qualifying for the French Grand Prix and this was raced for the first time in Germany. Hockenheim also saw Ligier progress to a slightly less sophisticated version of this evolution – the RS6A.

Finally, an RS6C version, featuring new camshafts, was available for both Williams and Ligier for the final two races of the season in Japan and Australia.'

RENAULT RS7 ENGINE

The engine that in 1995 powered both the William FW17s of Damon Hill and David Coulthard plus the Benetton 195s of Michael Schumacher and Johnny Herbert.

RS7:
2 Grand Prix: Brazil and Australia
2 wins
2 pole positions
2 fastest laps
33 points scored

RS7A:
4 Grand Prix: San Marino, Spain, Monaco and Canada
3 wins: San Marino, Spain and Canada
4 pole positions
2 fastest laps: Spain and Canada

RS7B:
4 Grand Prix: France, Great Britain, Germany and Hungary
4 wins
4 pole positions
4 fastest laps
72 points scored

RS7C:
7 Grand Prix: Belgium, Europe, Italy, Portugal, Pacific, Japan and Australia
7 wins
6 pole positions: Italy, Portugal, Europe, Pacific, Australia and Japan
6 fastest laps: Belgium, Portugal, Europe, Pacific, Australia and Japan
108 points scored

RS7 main characteristics:
Type: V10 (67 degrees)
Length: 623mm
Width: 540mm
Height (up to cylinder heads): 420mm
Weight: approximately 132kg, according to accessories
Cylinder heads in aluminium; cylinder block, crank case and timing cover in light aluminium
Four valves per cylinder

Air-valve timing
Electronic engine management and static ignition by Magneti-Marelli

Changes compared with the RS6:
All new cylinder heads
New cylinder block, built along similar lines to that of the RS6 but narrower and lower
New moving parts, not only as a result of the reduction in capacity compared with the RS6 but also because of certain design changes introduced with a view to reducing friction
New injection computer and new data logging unit developed in association with Magneti-Marelli
Electronically controlled throttle

Bernard Dudot: 'When Formula One's engine manufacturers collectively agreed to propose a reduction in cubic capacity to 3 litres to the FIA in May 1994, work on the Renault engine initially planned for 1995 was already at an advanced stage. Nevertheless, we took the decision to drop the original project, which was ill-suited to the latest regulation changes, and turned our attention instead to the development of an all-new engine. It was in fact based on a design closer in general structural terms to the RS6 of 1994 originally planned. Time was short and, rather than redesigning everything from scratch, we chose to focus our attention on producing a 3-litre engine to an extremely demanding brief.

Consequently, the RS7 was not just a 3-litre version of the RS6 but a genuine, all-new engine, which from its very first Grand Prix boasted a maximum engine speed of more than 1,000rpm – superior to that of the RS6 in its end-of-1994 specification. In the course of the 1995 season, the RS7 underwent three major evolutions. The first was introduced for the San Marino Grand Prix at Imola and concerned the timing and intake systems as well as revised bore and stroke dimensions. There was no increase in the maximum revs at this time. The second evolution went significantly further, however, and concentrated principally on the intake system. Maximum engine speeds went up by between 400

and 500rpm and the modifications had an appreciable effect on the overall performance of the RS7. I believe that it was at this moment that we pulled out a clear advantage over our main rivals. Not only was the resulting increase in power significant but, more importantly, it covered the entire useful rev band without the slightest compromise in terms of reliability. The third evolution, which saw the introduction of new camshafts, was available for the Belgian Grand Prix - that is, a full Grand Prix earlier than anticipated. The improvements at that time effectively allowed us to maintain the edge we had over our rivals from the halfway point in the season right through to the end of the championship. Like its predecessor, the RS7 engine proved remarkably reliable – although two incidents did end in race retirements. The first was in Argentina where David Coulthard was stopped by an electronic throttle calculator problem and the second was in Hungary where Michael Schumacher was sidelined by a problem with his high-pressure pump. Having said that, whether it be in qualifying or during a Grand Prix, the RS7 didn't suffer a single failure in the course of the 1995 season.'

RENAULT RS8 ENGINE

The engine that in 1996 powered both the Benetton-Renaults of Jean Alesi and Gerhard Berger and the Williams cars of Damon Hill and Jacques Villeneuve.

RS8:
5 Grand Prix: Australia, Brazil, Argentina, Europe and San Marino
5 wins
5 pole positions
83 points scored

RS8A:
3 Grand Prix: Monaco, Spain and Canada
1 win: Canada
2 pole positions: Spain and Canada
2 fastest laps: Monaco and Spain
30 points scored

Tune-up,
February 1990

RS8B:

8 Grand Prix: France, Great Britain, Germany, Hungary, Belgium, Italy, Portugal and Japan
6 wins: France, Great Britain, Germany, Hungary, Belgium, Italy, Portugal and Japan
7 fastest laps: France, Great Britain, Germany, Hungary, Belgium, Portugal and Japan
130 points scored

Main characteristics:
Type: V10 (67 degrees)
Length: 623mm
Width: 540mm
Height (up to cylinder head): 420.2mm
Weight: Approximately 132kg, according to accessories
Cylinder heads in aluminium; cylinder block, crank case and timing cover in light aluminium
Four valves per cylinder
Air-valve timing
Electronic engine management and static ignition by Magneti-Marelli

Changes compared to the RS7:
All new cylinder heads
New cylinder block, built along similar lines to that of the RS7 but lower
New bore/stroke ratio for moving parts
New Magneti-Marelli management

Bernard Dudot: 'Design work on the RS8 engine began relatively late in the 1995 season. Early on, this very ambitious project was redirected and today elements from preliminary engineering phases have made their appearance as the starting point for the RS9. The RS8 was eventually designed on the basis of engineering the RS7. By comparison the cylinder heads were redesigned and a new bore/stroke ratio implemented to enhance high revs and improve fuel intake.

By mutual agreement with our partners, we began the 1996 season on the basis of a tried-and-tested reliability, with the aim of establishing an advantage over our opponents for the first three Grand Prix of the season. The first three races were run in Australia and South America – too far from our workshops for us to be able to deal with any potential fall-off

in reliability affecting either the engine or the chassis. Moreover, the 1995/96 off-season was extremely short which did not give us enough time to incorporate initially as many features into the RS8 as we would have liked.

During the course of the 1996 season, the engine underwent three subsequent evolutions. Almost 3.5kg of weight was shed from the upper part of the engine in qualification for the Monaco Grand Prix and in competition for the Spanish Grand Prix. There were new camshafts and a redesigned oil-drainage circuit at the French Grand Prix and new exhausts in qualification for the Italian Grand Prix and in competition for the Portuguese Grand Prix.

Although this is an unusual occurrence at Renault Sport, the RS8 suffered three failures during the season. The first victim was Damon Hill, when he was leading the Monaco Grand Prix. Then it was Gerhard Berger leading the German Grand Prix and finally came the Hungarian Grand Prix with Gerhard Berger again. Renault Sport had not experienced such a problem since 1993, when Alain Prost was obliged to pull up with engine failure while in the lead in the Italian Grand Prix.'

RENAULT RS9 ENGINE:

The engine that powered the Williams cars of Jacques Villeneuve and Heinz-Harald Frentzen plus the Benettons of Jean Alesi and Gerhard Berger.

17 Grand Prix
9 wins: Brazil, Argentina, San Marino, Spain, Great Britain, Germany, Hungary, Austria and Luxembourg
13 pole positions: Australia, Brazil, Argentina, San Marino, Monaco, Spain, Great Britain, Germany, Belgium, Italy, Austria, Europe and Japan
11 fastest laps: Australia, Brazil, Argentina, San Marino, Germany, Hungary, Belgium, Austria, Luxembourg, Europe and Japan

Main characteristics:
Type: V10 (The V forming an angle of 71 degrees)

Length: 623mm
Width: 542mm
Height (up to cylinder head): 395mm
Weight: approximately 121kg, according to accessories
Cylinder heads in aluminium; cylinder block, crank case and timing cover in light aluminium
Four valves per cylinder
Air-valve timing
Electronic engine management and static ignition by Magneti-Marelli

Changes compared to the RS8:
All new cylinder heads
New cylinder block with a centre of gravity lowered by 14mm (opening of the V engine)
New moving parts
Significant weight reduction
Friction reduction
New engine acoustics

Jean-Francois Robin: 'The RS9 is a whole new engine. We channelled our efforts into the lowering of the centre of gravity, the weight and general architecture of the engine in order to put an even better model into our partners' cars.

In terms of oil circulation and cooling, we took all the knowledge gained during the trials of the RS7 and RS8 and brought it together in this new engine.

So as not to compromise the start of the season with a brand new engine, we asked Williams to make a car capable of taking the RS9 from mid-November. This enabled us to run 11,000km of trials before the first Grand Prix, thus confirming our legendary reliability.'

ACKNOWLEDGEMENTS

The author would like to thank:
Renault F1 Enstone and Paris for access to their image library and statistical database.
Sarah Sabin
Serena Santolamazza
Patrizia Spinelli
of Renault F1 for their assistance

Additional information:
Biographical:
 www.renaultf1.com
 www.grandprix.com
 www.8w.forix.com
Statistical:
 'The Renault F1 Drivers Story' Wake Upp Editions, France

Technical assistance:
Phil Rogers

Promotional assistance:
John Cowan
James Crofts
David Lucas
Kevin and Scott Mansell of Mansell Motor Sport

Illustrations:
Driver portraits of Bellof, Dumfries, Frentzen and Wurz supplied by Empics.
Driver portraits of Streiff, Hesnault, Capelli, Alliot, Barnard and Lagorce, and images on pages 11, 19, 33 and 82-3 supplied by LAT Photographic.
All other images are copyright F1 Renault.

Jean-Pierre Jabouille, Dutch GP,
31 August 1980